THE GRUESOME, DISGUSTING, AND ABSOLUTELY VILE

GROSS-O-PEDIA

THE GRUESOME, DISGUSTING, AND ABSOLUTELY VILE

GROSS-O-PEDIA

A Startling Collection of Repulsive Trivia You Won't Want to Know!

Rachel Federman

Skyhorse Publishing

Illustration credits on page 251

Skyhorse Publishing books may be purchased in bulk at special discounts for sales promotion, corporate gifts, fund-raising, or educational purposes. Special editions can also be created to specifications. For details, contact the Special Sales Department, Skyhorse Publishing, 307 West 36th Street, 11th Floor, New York, NY 10018 or info@skyhorsepublishing.com.

Skyhorse® and Skyhorse Publishing® are registered trademarks of Skyhorse Publishing, Inc.®, a Delaware corporation.

www.skyhorsepublishing.com

10 9 8 7 6 5 4 3 2 1

Library of Congress Cataloging-in-Publication data is on file.

ISBN: 978-1-62087-184-3

Printed and bound in China by South China Printing Co. Ltd

Dedication

For my fifth-grade teacher, Mr. McInerney, who pushed us way beyond our comfort zone in a magical classroom where we were encouraged to experiment, learn from failure, face our fears, and prioritize true growth over outward measures of success—an approach to teaching that was rare then and, thanks to dwindling funds for public education and current testing mandates, is now all but extinct.

CONTENTS

I get really easily grossed out. So easily—and dramatically—in fact, that I used to faint because of it. The first time was when our amazing fifth-grade teacher, Mr. McInerney, mentioned that we'd be dissecting a sheep's eye. Or maybe he just had a sheep's eye in a jar of formaldehyde. I only heard the first part of the sentence, but I don't think I myself ever laid eyes on the eye of the ewe.

I also lost consciousness briefly when he told us to collect cells to examine under the microscope by running a little wooden stick against the inside of our cheeks. I woke up to the sound of Mr. McInerney's voice asking, "Are you with us?" I was, but it was touch and go from there — through junior high and most of high school. In chorus, I once fell off the back riser during a holiday show while the rest of the choir finished singing Billy Joel's "And so It Goes." I don't even remember what it was that initially bothered me. My mom heard the thud of my head hitting the stage but didn't realize I was missing until the end of the song. Another time, I ended up in the nurse's office after reading a story in English class about a boy who swam underwater so long that his blood vessels burst.

Some people said what I had was a "real thing," and that it even had a name: blood-injury phobia (see *You Look a Little Pale*, pg. 84). Others just said I had a weak stomach. In biology lab, everyone around me wielded scalpels and seemed remarkably brave, while just I prayed for the bell to ring. I started to realize something funny, which was that hearing disturbing stories bothered me more than actually seeing something gross. It was my imagination, in the end, that really got the best of me.

After a while, the other kids started to look out for me. They let the teacher know when a news topic of someone finding a severed hand in the woods or Ozzy Osbourne chewing the heads off bats came up that maybe they should change the subject—either that or give me a pass to study hall. They'd tell me not to look at a slide showing a giraffe carcass being torn apart by leopards. Sometimes they caught me in time, and I put my head between my knees before I blacked out. Most of the teachers understood. I learned to get used to spinning rooms. And to sit by the exit signs.

Family members joked that after all that fainting, I'd grow up to be a surgeon. That didn't happen. But I did grow up to write a book about blood, guts, gaping wounds, giant cockroaches, earthworm soup, flying mucus, belly lint, and dead bodies piling up on Mount Everest.

So here's the million-dollar question:
Did I faint during the writing of this book?

I did not—although that would have made for a good story. But the truth is, I finally outgrew the phobia when I realized that what actually made me faint wasn't the sense of disgust or horror I felt when picturing the pile of severed limbs at Gettysburg—it was the fear that I *would* faint.

Here's what actually happened: You faint when your brain doesn't get enough oxygen. For some people, a drop in blood pressure is the body's natural response to seeing blood or, in my case, hearing about it. Scientists aren't sure why, though some think that it may have once been adaptive, causing people to faint in battle or during an attack, to be passed over for dead by the enemy. The drop in blood pressure leads to light-headedness and, if it persists, to fainting, where you end up in a horizontal position and blood levels are restored to your brain. So basically, fainting is the body's way of correcting the oxygen deficit to the brain. When you think of it that way, it's not as scary as it seems—as long as you don't bang your head too hard when you land.

For me, fainting became a bad habit. When I heard about some guy getting a hole in his carotid artery, before I even had *time* to think about the blood spurting out, I started to panic about fainting. My blood pressure would drop, the room would spin, and away I'd go. It was a self-fulfilling prophecy. To train myself out of that cycle, I had to stop worrying that I would faint. Eventually I did. Now I don't even have to sit by the exit signs—but it took a while.

So that's a good lesson for all of you out there who just can't get enough of blood and guts or the ones, like me, who tend to feel a little woozy just hearing the plot of a Stephen King novel. The 32nd president, Franklin Delano Roosevelt, nailed it when he said, "The only thing we have to fear is fear itself." It's an interesting physiological phenomenon that the fear of something happening might make that very thing more likely to happen. The trick is not to be afraid of what might happen, and then chances are high that the thing won't. Like making a mistake at your piano recital, failing a test, ruining a friendship, or letting down your teammates by missing a crucial goal.

In order *not* to fail, you have to be okay with failing. It's paradoxical. But you can't trick yourself into believing that it's okay to faint, or fail, or fall down on the ice, or give a terrible speech. You can't say, "Okay, yeah, it's fine, no problem; I don't mind getting a big giant F. Now, hurry up universe, Give me an A." You have to really be *okay* with falling with a big, giant thud right in the middle of your solo piece at the end of the year ballet recital. Even if your crush is in the audience. Because, as long as you don't get seriously hurt, it really is okay.

Luckily for now, all you have to do is read about gross horrible stuff in the comfort of your own living room with a nice fluffy pillow under your head. (Don't give any thought to the fact that the pillow is teeming with dust mites.) Read about icky animals, killer insects, piles of earwax, hearts preserved in jars, and people swallowing live mice.

Let your imagination take you where hopefully your feet never will.

Read on, brave Grossophiles!

BIZARRE CUISINE

Why is caviar considered the height of gross food? We eat eggs all the time—on their own or in cakes, cookies, quiche, and in a million other places. Is the problem we have with caviar the number of offspring all in one place? Or the fact that they come from fish? The color? In South America, quail eggs are common—they're smaller than the ones from chickens but taste essentially the same. Still you may find yourself turning your nose up if offered one on top of a hot dog in Columbia or pickled in Vietnam. Funny how much taste depends on custom and familiarity. Many Asian dishes, such as those that include canine, strike Westerners as barbaric; meanwhile we have no problem with chomping down on a cow, an animal treated as sacred in India. Still other dishes seem merely gross rather than cruel or disrespectful—you won't see many in the Western world run to all-you-can-eat python, scorpion, dried jellyfish, or bear paw. (We'll stick with the pupu platter!)

Protein Power

You thought beef and tofu were high in protein? It's true they've got a little, but if you really want to stock up, you're looking in the wrong place. In fact, you might not need to look in the kitchen at all. How about the basement, attic, or garage instead? Winding your way down to a cold, dark cellar? You're getting warmer: spiders, houseflies, and grasshoppers are where it's at.

Did You Know? *Dried grasshopper-stuffed tacos are called* chapulines. *You can get them in New York City at the Mexican restaurant Toloache.*

Walks Like a Chicken, Tastes Like a Chicken

How many things that *aren't* chicken are described as tasting *like* chicken?

- Chicken cutlets made of soy protein
- Wendy's chicken sandwich (contains beef)
- Frogs
- Goose
- Pigeon
- Alligator
- Rabbit
- Iguana

> **Be an Expert!** *Feeling hesitant about taking the leap to insects? In Leviticus 11, the Bible advises people to "Eat any kind of locust, katydid, cricket or grasshopper."*

If you're afraid to try something exotic, maybe you don't have to be. There's a pretty good chance it will —you guessed it!—taste like chicken.

> **Did You Know?** *For your next big event, you can hire a New York City-based band named Tastes Like Chicken.*

MOUTHWATERING FRIGHTS

Keep that extra spoon that you never use handy. You may just need it to gag yourself after sampling some of these mouthwatering delights from around the world:

- Ants' eggs
- Boiled locusts
- Chocolate-covered cockroaches
- Crayfish head
- Dog liver
- Dung beetles
- Flour beetle larvae
- Garlic waxworms
- Grilled snake
- Longicorn larvae
- Rat meat
- Rattlesnake salad
- Raw worms
- Roasted guinea pigs
- Seahorses
- Spiced giant waterbugs (3 inches long!)

Oh, and let's not forget dry-roasted crickets, which we're told taste just like smoked nuts!
(Which, of course, begs the question:

Why not just eat smoked nuts instead?)

I Scream for Ice Cream

Sushi has become a hot trend, with or without the raw fish, and the sea lovers among you may even enjoy seaweed alone for a nice crunchy, mineral-filled snack. But most everyone has surely consumed seaweed in an unlikely place: ice cream. See "carrageenan" listed on the back of your favorite tub of Ben & Jerry's? It's extracted from boiled seaweed. (So, maybe you're not as picky as you thought.)

It's All in a Name

Horsetail tangle, bladderwrack, and sea otter's cabbage sound more exotic than they are. Turns out, they're all types of edible seaweed.

Everything in Moderation—Even Fly Larvae

Swear you'll never eat a bug? Chances are you already have—hundreds of them! The U.S. government allows 30 insect parts for every 100 grams of peanut butter. Similar legal amounts of accidental ingredients apply to all processed food. (Hey, everybody makes mistakes!). *The*

Food and Drug Administration Defect Levels Handbook lists all this stuff as passable, in moderation: mold, insect infestation, rodent hairs, worms, excrement, fly eggs, and maggots. So don't worry about a stray rat hair dropping in on your Fluffernutter; there are bugs aplenty put in food on purpose. (See *chapulines,* pg. 16.)

Did You Know? *On average, most of us swallow about a pound of insect parts every year.*

Champagne and Fish Eggs

Caviar—the go-to disgusting food for various dares and challenges—are fish eggs: unpasteurized sturgeon roe to be exact. Is it the fact that they're uncooked that's repulsive? Or maybe it's just the visual—kind of like how one ant alone is fine, but hundreds teeming around the dropped lollipop is horrid. A Japanese company sells edible fake caviar that is pretty convincing. Help endangered fish populations: eat more fake caviar!

Mmmm...Civet Droppings

Forget Sumatra, when it comes to quality coffee, civet droppings are all the rage. The beans are called Kopi Luwak, but don't let the name fool you. They come from the backsides of civets (see *In the Know,* pg. 22). And don't worry, they're fermented by the time they're dropped off. You can pay up to $600 per pound for these partially digested berries. According to the *New York Times*, they are reported to be "smooth, chocolaty, and devoid of any bitter aftertaste."

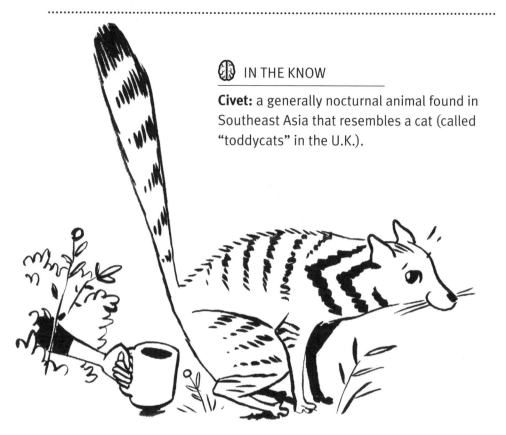

IN THE KNOW

Civet: a generally nocturnal animal found in Southeast Asia that resembles a cat (called "toddycats" in the U.K.).

The Bone Truth

You may know that Worcestershire sauce contains anchovies, but why stop there? The fish's bones are also thrown in for good measure. (As far as we can tell, anchovies themselves don't even need bones. Why they feel compelled to bring them along to the Worcestershire sauce is anybody's guess.)

A Single Scoop Will Do

Rainy summers in England led to this innovative cozy cone as an alternative to traditional frozen treats served from ice-cream trucks. Aunt Bessie's "Mash Van" tours the U.K., serving up a familiar combo with a twist: mashed potatoes, sausages, and peas inside a cone traditionally reserved for ice cream. Instead of dinner for dessert, why not try it the other way around?

Tails, You Die

A fugu fish (also known as a puffer fish or blowfish) is sometimes toxic, but that doesn't hurt its reputation as a delicacy in Japan and, increasingly, in the United States. Its effect on approximately 300 unlucky people a year, however, is rather *indelicate*. Victims croak—and we don't mean

---

From a consumer advisory on the Food and Drug Administration's website:
"The liver, gonads (ovaries and testes), intestines, and skin of some puffer fish contain the toxins tetrodotoxin and/or saxitoxin. **These toxins are 1,200 times more deadly than the poison cyanide** and can affect a person's central nervous system. There are no known antidotes for these toxins. Puffer fish must be cleaned and prepared properly so the organs containing the toxins are carefully removed and do not cross-contaminate the flesh of the fish. These toxins cannot be destroyed by cooking or freezing."

---

imitate the sound a frog makes. Instead, consumers get snuffed out, breathe their last breath, hit the junkyard, land in their final resting place. After eating this fish, some people go swim with it.

Hmm. We think that puts puffer fish pretty safely in the "not worth it" category when it comes to extreme eating.

Biting Back

If mosquito season is making you hungry, you're not alone. Marc Dennis, founder of *Insects Are Food*, believes that mealworm French fries and chocolate-dipped crickets are examples of "what sushi was two decades ago"—rather exotic, but about to go mainstream. As defined on his website, "entomophagy" is the practice

Did You Know? *There's a popular dish in Nepal made from bee pupae. It's called bakuti and tastes like nuts. Sometimes you feel like bakuti, sometimes you don't.*

of eating insects, including tarantulas and centipedes. Dennis believes a bug diet is nutritional, sustainable, and delicious and simply requires changing preconceived Western mindsets about what constitutes a meal, given that eating insects is common practice the world over.

Grubby Grub

Need some inspiration for your newfound love of entomophagy (see **Biting Back**, pg. 24)? Get into the practice of eating insects with *The Eat-a-Bug Cookbook: 33 ways to cook grasshoppers, ants, water bugs, spiders, centipedes, and their kin*, by David George Gordon. One online reviewer originally bought it as a prank but ended up enjoying the recipes. I wonder what

Did You Know? *The Insect Club in Washington, DC is now gone, but it once served up some really fine mealworms. (Don't worry—they tasted like chicken.)*

dinner guests say? "I'll have the thigh. No the other thigh. No the other thigh." *Bugs for Lunch* by Margery Facklam and Sylvia Long is a rhyming picture book on the subject just for kids.

Odd Combos

Sometimes preferred foods alone aren't inherently gross, but the combination of unlikely flavors is not everyone's cup of vinegar tea. Need some unusual snack ideas?

How about:
- Peanut butter and mayo
- Beans and chocolate
- Pickles and peanut butter
- Popcorn and mustard
- Ketchup on pancakes

(We found people who liked each one of the above specialized blends; though no one person could honestly say he or she liked *all* of them. Do you?)

WORLD'S STRANGEST ICE CREAM FLAVORS:

- Cold sweat
- Caviar
- Spaghetti and cheese
- Lobster
- Guinness

- Horse
- Sea slug
- Bacon and egg
- Wasabi
- Avocado

(To the makers of the above concoctions—Guys, you're kind of missing the entire point! If we wanted something that tasted like an avocado, we'd eat an avocado! Not ice cream. This reminds me of the *Saturday Night Live* sketch, where the actors are eating ice cream that tastes like yogurt and keep saying, "I can't believe it's not yogurt!" How would you sell the stuff on the list above? "I can't believe it's not lobster! Twice the fat! Twice the calories! And half the taste.")

Did You Know? *The Japanese eat ice cream made with squid ink. At least you know you're getting the real thing! (Oops—cancel that. You can't be sure you're getting squid. Turns out the ink is sometimes extracted from its cousin the cuttlefish.)*

You Look Lovely, but You Smell Awful!

Hair dye in a box for $10 is a modern invention. Years ago, changing your hair color was quite a process. A hairdresser slave in ancient Rome used these items in various combinations for their fickle masters' tresses: rotten leeches, squid ink, pigeon droppings, bile, and human pee.

Just a Hint of Swine

How about a little bonbon post dinner on your trip to Madrid? Just steer clear of *Mantecado de Artesania*—along with wheat flour, sugar, and cinnamon, the special after-tapas treat serves up the delectable taste of...pork butter—a fat commonly used for desserts in the land of the sun. You planned to *make* a pig of yourself at dessert time, not *consume* one.

> " *A corpse is meat gone bad.*
> *Well and what's cheese?*
> *Corpse of milk.*"
> —JAMES JOYCE

Loosen Your Zipper

Foie gras literally means "fat liver," so it may come as no surprise that the delicacy made from goose or duck liver is created by unnaturally inflating the organ through over-feeding, a practice that began in ancient Egypt.

Sloppy Toppings

What's your favorite pizza topping? If you're like most Americans, it's pepperoni. Or maybe bell peppers, mushrooms, or extra cheese. Well, the Japanese are rather unique when it comes to pizza, asking for pizza makers to slide a squid or eel on top.

Did You Know? *There are some rather bizarre pizza toppings sliding down the throats of people even closer to home. Besides the usual pepperoni and extra cheese, here are some creative ideas from Recipe Pizza: "The World's Favorite Pizza Recipe website": avocado (wrong texture, in our opinion), alfalfa sprouts (too much work), walnuts (maybe on chocolate pizza!), lobster (this sounds messier than even we can imagine)...*

Octopus Vulgaris

Television doctor Dr. Oz has a suggestion for viewers who want to cut back on their red meat intake: grilled octopus. Apparently, he grew up on the stuff. He says to boil it with some parsley, tomatoes, and wine then freeze until you're

Be an Expert! *Disgust is a useful feeling to have—but it may have evolved as a way to keep us from getting sick. Think of the things you're disgusted by: many of them could carry viruses or bacteria.*

ready to grill. Serve with a Dijon mustard vinaigrette. Let your guests guess what they're eating. Then tell them where you got the recipe and that the eight-legged sucker has lots of vitamin B-12. (And the octopus does, too!)

Score for Scorpion Lovers

Feeling squeamish about trying scorpion? We were, too, until we found out that the poison is removed from the scorpion's stinger once it's been cooked. *Ohhhh! Why didn't you tell us?* We would have chowed down on the death stalker years ago. Beijing is full of all kinds of scorpion delights, but you even can get it closer to home. In Los Angeles, the restaurant Typhoon serves it fried on toast, fully intact (except the poison, of course).

Embryonic Delicacy

Your parents may be careful now to buy eggs with lots of qualifiers on the package: organic, vegetarian fed, cage-free chickens, and so on. But there's one thing that all the eggs we buy and eat have in common — they are unfertilized. The chicken laid them, but before the rooster had a chance to come along and do his part, they were whisked away to our supermarket shelves.

Okay, now that we've got that straight cut, let's cut to a dish called balut, a favorite repast in the Philippines. These eggs *have been fertilized!* They're allowed to grow for over a week just as nice as can be until they're boiled alive and served up fetal style. They're dead by the time they reach your plate, thankfully (unlike these unfortunate fellows, see **Nosedive,** pg. 33). Inside the eggshell you'll find the tiny duck fetus, alongside the yolk. Even if you don't make it to the Philippines anytime soon, you can give it a try at a restaurant in New York City called Maharlika Filipino Moderno.

Did You Know? *Eating raw fish such as salmon can transfer parasites to the consumer that will grow into tapeworms longer than the consumer. Supermarkets are becoming savvier to the process of using tweezers to pick parasites off fish before stocking the shelves. The FDA recommends freezing fish before consuming it raw.*

Hungry-Man Dinner

A man once swallowed 53 toothbrushes, two razors—and that wasn't all. The doctors also found 157 other inedible objects in this man's stomach at a single time. On the plus side, he was clean-shaven and didn't have any cavities! Guess picky eaters should stop complaining about being forced to eat a piece or two of broccoli.

Nosedive

Eating raw fish is so last century. But what about eating raw fish that are still alive? People do it. In some countries, it's considered a special treat. Most live fish going down the hatch are small enough to swallow whole, but the Chinese serve a rather large fish that survives being deep fried in the kitchen and making its way all the way to your plate, where it greets you still alive and breathing. Talk about a lively meal. As the French say, *Bon appétit!* Or perhaps the Jewish toast is more fitting: *La Chaim*! (Meaning, to life!)

Feline Dreams

In 2007, surgeons found a ten-pound hairball inside the stomach of a teenager—yet another reason not to groom your cat with your tongue.

IN THE KNOW

Pica: a disorder in which the sufferer has a craving for things that are inedible. Some specific examples:
- *Xylophagia*—eating wooden toothpicks
- *Geophagia*—eating clay or dirt
- *Amylophagia*—eating laundry starch and paste

Say Cheese!

On the island of Sardinia, there's a kind of pecorino cheese that is purposely left out to rot until it is covered in maggots. It's intentionally eaten that way, with live maggots jumping in every direction! *Formaggio Marcio* is now illegal but still popular on the underground market. We wonder if the word sardonic—a kind of dark sarcasm—has any connection to this maggot-filled cheese.

Slippery Devils

A woman in Fairfield, Connecticut had a surprising discovery when she went to cook seven eels for the Night of the Seven Fishes celebration. One was still alive and looking back at her, perhaps praying desperately for a Night of Six instead.

Mold—the Good, the Bad, and the Ugly

Eat your fruit, but not if it's squishier than a pile of maggots (unless you're on the island of Sardinia, see **Say Cheese!** above) and starting to grow a gray fungus called mold. Is mold ever okay to eat? The answer is yes. Moldy cheeses, like Gorgonzola, are considered by many to be a culinary treat. The bacteria that is injected into the cheese to create the bluish moldy veins is also the bacteria found on smelly feet.

Is that Blood in My Pudding?

Is blood pudding as medieval as it sounds? That depends. First of all, it's more of a sausage than what we think of as pudding. According to the BBC, blood pudding is pigs' blood mixed with onions, oatmeal, barley, flour, pork fat, and various herbs and it's quite a popular breakfast item in the land of fish and chips. There is actually even a veggie version available made by Real Lancashire Black Pudding Company. It's called V Pud, and the creators took special pains to "simulate the properties of blood".

Did You Know? Moldy cheese has its own official day: October 9.

OUTLANDISH ANIMAL LAND

Putting the "ew" in Zoology! You don't have to look any farther than *Animal Planet* to see some of the yuckiest stuff around.

Banana Slugs

These slimy suckers can grow up to nearly a foot long, but true to their name, they don't make tracks very quickly, so you'd have no trouble peeling away from them. Their most distasteful feature is the mucus that oozes out of them for protection. Just make sure you don't mistake them for their edible namesakes: one lick of this mollusk's underbelly and your tongue will go numb.

Giant Squid

It sounds squishy, and it is. This mysterious sea creature is mostly muscle and an invertebrate, meaning that it has no hard skeleton. Despite its impressive size (the heaviest nearly breaks the scales at 2,000 pounds), it floats easily because of the ammonia in its muscle, which is lighter than water. These slimy suckers have plenty of everything: eight arms, three hearts, two tentacles—both much longer than their body, the largest eyes in the animal world, and up to 300 suckers to grab onto prey. If you could get up close, you'd see that each sucker is lined with loads of tiny teeth, close to 50 on each one. All together, you're talking about 15,000 choppers.

Tattle-Tail

People always want to know which is the biggest animal... so naturally, being a *Gross-o-pedia* reader, you will want to know which animal is responsible for the biggest poop. And maybe even how big the poop itself is. Well, the blue whale takes first prize for biggest animal. Are they also number one for number two? That's hard to say. They usually have the runs, which makes the output rather difficult to measure. Still, we can assure you that whale's tail leaves one giant whale trail.

Crooked Shark Poop

If sharks aren't creepy enough, with their ability to smell a single drop of blood in 25 gallons of water, they also poop in an unusual way—it comes out in a spiral! Scientists who study fossilized poop found spiral coprolite and identified it as coming from a shark because their intestines have a matching shape.

🧠 IN THE KNOW

Coprolite—fossilized poop

I Want to Suck Your Blood…
Using an Anticoagulating Agent

How do vampire bats get their victims to spill their blood? Well, they have an anticoagulating agent in their saliva, which prevents the blood from clotting.

Unpopular Scavengers

Why do vultures get such a bad rap for preying on wounded animals or on those who have already been partially eaten? It seems like a gentler method of survival than attacking a perfectly healthy animal in the prime of its life. Maybe it's the way that they creep up on victims or peck at their eyeballs. And, of course, they *do* pee on themselves to cool off and regurgitate food into the mouths of their young, so, on second thought, the ostracized vultures fit squarely in the confines of a book on gross stuff!

> **Be an Expert!**
> Vultures have bald heads so that they don't collect blood and bits of dead flesh in their feathers after they poke around inside a carcass.

This Means War

The Portuguese man-of-war looks like a jellyfish, but it's actually a colony of invertebrates all clumped together. The tentacles can extend down to as much as 165 feet underwater. If that's not scary enough, washed-up dead men-of-war have still been known to sting people!

One-Stop Shopping

The chicken is an efficient little animal. Its underside has only one hole, and all these things come out of it: eggs, poop, and pee. (Sperm travels through the same shoot—opposite direction.) Here's hoping there aren't any traffic jams!

IN THE KNOW

Zoophobia: this one's easy to remember, as it means fear of animals. We're all scared of tigers or snakes that might kill us, and that's a good thing. A zoophobic is the friend whose heart starts pounding when your mini poodle wakes up from his nap.

Squirmy Worms

Pinworms grow in your intestines and are very contagious. Can you guess which part of your body they come out of? Think for a minute. The intestines lead to...your butt—which means that the worms may show up in your underwear or in the toilet if you get infected. They are little white stringlike fellows less than half an inch long. The females go to work while you are asleep, planting thousands of eggs around your butt skin. You'll start to itch, but it's best not to scratch. There are effective medications, but it can take quite a while to completely wipe out an infestation. Washing your hands is the best prevention.

Trippy Fish

When snorkeling off the coast of Florida, don't be drawn in by a piranha's beguiling smile. These river beasts can easily rip off skin with their teeth. Its African relative, the Goliath tigerfish, has even been known to eat crocodiles.

IN THE KNOW

Herpetophobia: fear of reptiles, especially lizards and snakes

Lots of Snot

As gross animals go, giraffes don't even rank, except for their 18-inch tongues, which work double duty by chewing leaves and giving their nostrils a clean sweep. Ever heard of touching your tongue with your nose? These guys keep riding right on inside and then stay awhile.

Two Heads Are Better than One

On various occasions, unusual snakes, calves, and turtles have all appeared with two heads on one body. There was once even a calf born with eight legs and two tails, although it did at least have the decency to limit his head count to

Did You Know? The famed horny toad, celebrated outdoor pet of many a Texas child, is really a lizard. But that's not the exciting part. These lizards can squirt blood from their eyes!

one. On the other hand, the two-headed blind Brazilian snake has only one cranium, along with a misleading tail that also resembles one. Turns out the reptile's not blind, either; however it *can* move in either direction—heads or tails.

Porta-Umbrella

Shower much? An alligator in British Guiana once grew a tree on its back. At least he didn't have to look for a shady spot to rest.

> **Did You Know?** *In the United Kingdom, skunks are occasionally domesticated (kept as house pets). Since 2006, taking out their scent glands is against the law, so think twice before bringing one home and letting him sleep in your bed. These gentle creatures, who eat seeds, berries, fruit, and insects, will issue a warning before spraying in self-defense, however. So if you see a raised tail, run the other way.*

Smell You Later

We've all seen it happen. We may look away and pretend we don't notice, just like we do when our math teacher has his fly down. But still, we have to ask the question: Why do dogs smell each other's privates upon initial greeting? As *Psychology Today* points out, given that dogs can sniff out cocaine and dead bodies, "Why would a dog need to stick his nose directly into another dog's snout, genitals, and nether regions to garner social information? Couldn't he do that at a 'safer' distance?" The answer to this is inconclusive, as dog experts don't agree on this rather boorish behavior. Some say a face-to-face greeting can be seen as confrontational, while others say canines collect more information from going where no man dares to go.

Did You Know? *Dogs are champion smellers. Compared to the measly five percent of your brain devoted to figuring out that you stepped in something other than mud, at least a third of a dog's brain is dedicated to olfactory stuff.*

IN THE KNOW

Olfactory: it sounds like something you'd find in an abandoned mill town, but olfactory actually means having to do with your sense of smell, from the Latin *olfacere* (to smell).

Bite-Size Reptile

A rattlesnake was no match for Rodney Fluery, who, in 1971, killed one by biting it.

Prehistoric Horror

The 2007 discovery of a fossilized giant scorpion claw has led scientists to believe that spiders and other objects of our disgust had been even bigger than previously believed. As Dr. Simon Braddy from the University of Bristol put it, "This is an amazing discovery. We have known for some time that the fossil record yields monster millipedes, super-sized scorpions, colossal cockroaches, and jumbo dragonflies, but we never realized, until now, just how big some of these ancient creepy-crawlies were. We think the claws on this creature would have been powerful enough to rip someone to shreds."

Glow in the Dark

Scorpions can glow in the dark. If you have an ultraviolet light, you'll be able to see them. They're also poisonous, though—so stand at a good distance. We'd rather stand as far as possible away—maybe even light years away—by gazing safely at the Scorpio constellation in the night sky. (If you're more adventurous, maybe you'd like to taste one. See *Score for Scorpion Lovers*, pg. 31.)

Sea Cucumber

Such a harmless name, and some people do eat them, but it's what *they* eat that's rather disturbing: a mixture of dead animal matter and feces. They're also called sea slugs— even less appealing, isn't it?

Dining in

A hagfish eats its prey from the inside out (by slipping inside through the prey's mouth or any other opening that's big enough). It also has a rather interesting way of protecting itself: it produces slime that chokes its predators.

The Big Gulp

Have you ever used the term "big mouth" for a friend who can't keep secrets? Well, he or she probably has nothing on the gulper eel—his entire head is basically one huge chomper.

> **Did You Know?** Hippos fling around their own poop and pee with their tails, to mark their territories and show others who is boss. Couldn't they just get one of those corny mugs with the words "World's Greatest Boss"?

Ocean Whopper

In the Bible, Jonah spends three days inside the belly of a whale. Finally God ordered the whale to upchuck the prophet. If it had been a blue whale, Jonah could have fit neatly inside a blood vessel. A blue whale's blood vessels are wider than your entire body!

The Last Supper—as in, the One You Just Had

When a wolf returns to the pack from a solo romp, the other wolves lick its mouth to see if any prey has been captured and eaten. But that's not the gross part. If any prey is detected, the swallower is supposed to share by regurgitation. Now that's *grossitating*! Our guess is that they eat pretty fast at least. The expression "to wolf it down" has to come from somewhere.

It's Raining Snakes

It's a bird, it's a plane, it's a...flying snake! Their official name is chrysopelea, but the truth is, these fellows don't actually fly. Instead, they crawl to the end of a tree branch and launch. They do a good enough job of gliding by twisting their bodies back and forth between an S and a C shape that they appear to be flying as they make their way down.

Double-Duty Sucker

Octopuses use one of their arms in the process of reproduction. The hectocotylus arm is particularly flexible — that's the one males use to enter the female cavity and fertilize the eggs. But wait, there's more. Some kinds of octopuses up the grossness ante by leaving part of that arm behind. The female receives the sperm, along with a sacrificial limb. (The male dies soon after, so perhaps the amputation is not a big a deal in the overall scheme of things.)

WICKEDLY WEIRD NEWS

"A Giant Mutant Rat" and "The Dead Body under the Christmas Tree"—these headlines are horrible, so why do we keep reading? Blood and gore in black and white—it's the modern-day version of watching gladiators fight. There's just some primal hankering in humans for blood and disgust that attracts and repels us at the same time. Kind of like a magnet if the two sides overlapped. But then it wouldn't be a magnet. Okay, we need a better metaphor here. In the meantime, press on through the weird and terrible stranger-than-fiction truth! And be glad you're not in print, at least for these stories.

Monster Rat

New York City subways are notoriously rat infested, but Jose Rivera was in for a surprise when he came upon a group of gigantic, mutant white rats in Brooklyn, where he was working for the housing authority. He ended up stabbing and killing one with a pitchfork. A wildlife expert believed the super-size rodent was likely a Gambian pouched rat that had once been a house pet (which, in our estimation, is even weirder than the image of one running loose outside).

Something's Buggin' Me

In 2004, *National Geographic* published a report called "For Most People, Eating Bugs Is Only Natural". Examples throughout history and even the modern age are plentiful, from Aristotle's advice on harvesting cicadas—full of eggs, if you're lucky—to the coconut and ginger dragonflies favored in Bali today. (See **Bizarre Cuisine** for lots of great recipe ideas.)

Nailed the Landing

A car crash ended the reign of former long-nail queen Lee Redmond, who had not trimmed her nails for 30 years. Before it snapped off, the longest nail scratched in at just under 3 feet. Today's record holder, Chris Walton, has a combined 19 feet and 19 inches. But that doesn't stop her from texting her friends. She just uses her knuckles. (Hmmm, hard to picture, but if you say so (or we should say IUSS =)

Have Mercy on the Mercy Flusher

On the online zine The Poop Report "Your #1 Source for #2," one user posted to say he was going to stop employing the "courtesy flush" because it did not really have the intended effect, instead, merely signaling that the flusher knows he or she stink bombed the place but can't do anything about it. Why waste water just to be polite?

Rude Awakening

A Russian woman named Fagilyu Mukhametzyanov woke up from a deep sleep at a funeral—her own! She was lying in a coffin, mistaken for dead, while loved ones paid their respects. Sadly, the story takes yet another strange twist. The shock of waking up in such an odd state of affairs led to a heart attack that killed poor Fagilyu Mukhametzyanov.

Automatic Slither Machine

An unsuspecting customer in a Spanish bank once reached for cash and found a snake crawling out of his ATM instead. Bank managers brought the lost serpent to a shelter, and the man finally received his greenbacks.

She Meets Herself Coming and Going

In Chongqing, China, there's a waitress named Wang Fang whose feet point backward (her toes are behind her).

Not Exactly Airborne

A woman once tried to bring a dead guy on a plane. She thought that sunglasses and a wheelchair would do the trick in getting him through security, but his silence started to arouse suspicion. That's a whole lotta baggage, in our opinion.

Don't Keep Your Trash Heap

People hoard all kinds of things, from clothes, to papers, to kitchen supplies. Some even hoard garbage. (Yuck! Why on Earth would anyone want to do that?) In 2007, the daytime talk show host Oprah Winfrey conducted a massive removal from one hoarder's home that included 75 tons of garbage alone.

Did You Know? *In 2010, a Chicago couple was found buried alive under all the trash they'd collected. Guess they really devoted themselves to their collection.*

Out with a Bang

In 2010, an Irish man named Michael Faherty died of apparent spontaneous combustion. Doctors were puzzled, but believed that it may have had something to do with excessive consumption of alcohol leading to a buildup of flammable oil in the blood. We can easily imagine what the priest said about poor Mr. Faherty in his eulogy: "He was here one day and then boom—just like that—he was gone."

Don't Let Them Get Away

Combine an interest in scatology with obsessive record-keeping and you've got the *Poo Log* by Josh Richman and Anish Sheth, M.D. As they write in the book's introduction: "Let's face it. There is no substitute for the hard (hopefully not *too* hard) facts." So get all the variations from Camouflage Poo to the Déjà Poo to Number Three ("liquid form"). Even the Hanging Chad deserves its time in the sun. Unless you've got the runs, run don't walk to pick up a copy of the book; you don't want to miss your chance to report on everything that exits.

Stick the Landing

Some people aren't kidding when they talk about projectile vomiting. The longest projectile hurl on record is 27 feet!

Hoist on Your Own Petard

A man in Montreal once hijacked a car, only to find out it was a diaper deliver service on a return trip and was full of dirty diapers. Talk about getting hoist on your own petard.

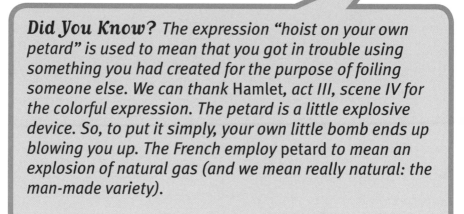

Did You Know? The expression "hoist on your own petard" is used to mean that you got in trouble using something you had created for the purpose of foiling someone else. We can thank Hamlet, act III, scene IV for the colorful expression. The petard is a little explosive device. So, to put it simply, your own little bomb ends up blowing you up. The French employ petard to mean an explosion of natural gas (and we mean really natural: the man-made variety).

Mannequins Make Better Friends

One Russian historian took his love of all things past a bit far. He exhumed bodies from the cemetery, dressed them up, and decorated his house with them.

Giddy up and Eat up—at the Same Time

Most Americans recoil at the idea of eating horse meat, but the U.S. Congress recently lifted a ban on funding inspections of the usually taboo food. That means that slaughterhouses may soon start welcoming Black Beauty and Seabiscuit as dinner guests.

I Wasn't Lovin' It

Just why do French fries at fast-food joints taste so good? Well, besides enough grease and salt to block a lifetime of arteries, your local burger haven fessed up that they often dip the oily spuds in sugar—just in case they were a little too healthy for your taste.

Oh, I Hope I Hope I Get a...Dead Body this Year?

"Dead woman found under Christmas tree, hidden under presents"—a strange, but real, headline that ran in December 2011. And we thought all the dead body pranks had ended two months before with Halloween.

Don't Drink the Water

Arsenic in the water is not just for murder mysteries anymore. A 2011 study by *Consumer Reports* found that levels of carcinogenic arsenic in several popular fruit juices were higher than FDA-approved levels for drinking water. A study by Dartmouth College found the same for rice. Sometimes invisible stuff is the scariest.

Super-Duper Libation

At White Castle in Louisville, Kentucky, you can find a chocolate milkshake with 1,680 calories (a unique speciality of Louisville). The drink itself is portable, but we're guessing that regular drinkers of these shakes may not be. We couldn't verify this fact on the Center for Disease Control website, but we thought we heard once that's exactly the same number of people whose pants exploded after drinking one.

Kiss and Tell, if You Can Still Talk

A kissing session once led to the accidental swallowing of false teeth–talk about an awkward first date!

Trapping Gas

"Under-Ease" are filter-equipped underwear that blocks the smell of farts from traveling to nearby nostrils. We wonder if those will cut down on hightails, too (when someone leaves the room to fart, then carries a trace of it back in with them). Experts tell us that if you're attempting a deliberate crop spray, you're better off with regular underwear or none at all.

It's Not too Late to Become a Mummy

Late-19th-century farmer Graham Hamrick of West Virginia turned the cadavers of two women from the local insane asylum into mummies, using a potion of vegetables, snakes, and a severed head. Okay, that sounds like the work of some random crackpot, right? Not an experiment that would gain widespread support. Think again. P.T. Barnum later featured the two modern mummies on a circus tour of Europe.

BLUE ICE

Toilet waste from an airplane is called "blue ice." The blue comes from the color of the disinfectant you see in the vacuum flusher. But talk about a euphemism. In our book, blue ice sounds rather nice,
"Would you like blue ice in your drink?"
"Sounds good to me...wait, *what?*"

It's a Long Way Down

A New York woman had an unwelcome visit one day, when a piece of frozen waste dropped on her house from a plane. It had the force to crash through the roof and landed—wait for it—in her bathroom. How did this happen, when waste isn't dumped midflight? Well, the hazardous waste is supposed to make the whole trip, but leaks do happen.

Did You Know? *Ever wondered what happens when you flush the toilet on a plane? Most people think it gets "dumped" over the ocean or lake. It's a bird, it's a plane, it's...flying crap! The truth is high-flying waste gets unloaded at the airport by the sanitation crew. So that's why it takes so long at the gate: someone didn't have enough fruit on vacay!*

Earth, Breaking Wind, and Fire

Disposable diapers have sure made life easier for moms and dads, reducing household pollution to a significant degree. But trash—no matter how repellant—doesn't just disappear. You know the children's book *Guess How Much I Love You*, where a pair of rabbits says they'd love each other up to the Moon and back? That's how far the number of diapers thrown out in the U.S. each year would stretch, if put end to end. But hopefully the diapers used in that experiment were super-absorbent. Otherwise that would be an awful lot of space goblins.

🧠 IN THE KNOW

Metaphor: a figure of speech that compares unlike things, substituting a word for something apparently unrelated to highlight an underlying connection.

Urban Legend or Real? You Decide: *A cockroach egg once made it from an envelope to a woman's tongue, where it hatched into a full-size roach.*

Whopping Whopper

A quarter pounder? That's nothing. How about getting your jaws around this one: the world's largest-ever sandwich clocked in at 6,991 pounds.

Talk about Losing Your Mind!

You've all heard the expression "running around like a chicken with its head cut off." Well, anyone who has seen a chicken farm can attest to the fact that chickens do run around for a minute or two after losing their heads, but one, Mike, "the Headless Wonder Chicken," lived for 18 months without that most crucial body part. Next time you feel particularly scatterbrained, searching for your backpack or cell phone, ask yourself, "Where's my head?" and then remember the chicken that really didn't have one.

FETID FESTIVALS

All around the world with rotten fish, cricket spit, moose droppings, and extreme body piercing. What are you waiting for? Plug your nose, cover your eyes, and let's go!

First One There Gets a Rotten Fish!

The popular pickled herring served at a traditional Scandinavian Christmas is nothing. In August, the Swedes participate in a festival called *Surströmming*, which means fermented herring. Everyone gathers together to eat stinky fish, on purpose. Don't worry, the rotten flesh is eaten with bread and raw onions to hide the taste and followed by vodka shots (for adults) to block out the memory. Not sure what you can do about the smell, though celebrants do have the common sense to eat outside so the stench can dissipate faster. Trying to imagine the taste? Think of rotten eggs mixed with butter that's gone bad and a touch of vinegar.

Coney Island Hot Dog Eating Contest

This 94-year-old tradition takes place every July 4th at Nathan's Famous in Brooklyn's legendary beachside amusement park. Takeru "Tsunami" Kobayashi holds the record for eating with gusto: in July of 2009, he shoveled 68 dogs (plus buns!) down his patriotic throat in just ten minutes. That's over 114 feet of food, which, when laid end to end, would be higher than a ten-story building.

Cricket-Spitting Contest

In 1990, Professor Tom Turpin at Purdue University began the annual "Bug Bowl" tradition. Along with cockroach races and an insect petting zoo, this entomologist has organized a popular cricket spitting competition for the past 11 years. Rules of the game? The bugs must be frozen and thawed prior to the event and remain fully intact throughout the spitting. According to the *Guinness Book of World Records*, the farthest a cricket has ever been spat is 32.5 feet. The chirpers used in the contest aren't ingested, but, in his classes, Professor Turpin encourages students to try a dry-roasted variety of crickets, along with fried mealworms, and other insect-based snacks. Sounds like he's not only an entomologist but an entomophagist as well. (See *Grubby Grub*, pg. 25.)

Moose Dropping Festival

Who says Alaska is not packed full of stuff to do? For starters, every July in Talkeetna, there used to be an entire festival based solely on moose droppings. Five thousand people flooded the area in 2009, eagerly joining in the moose-nugget toss and moose-nugget dropping contests and buying up moose-dropping jewelry. Things got too rowdy, however, and the Talkeetna Historical Society that sponsored it had to give the potty party the royal flush.

Vegetarian Festival

A vegetarian festival is the *last* place you'd expect to find spears stabbing through live flesh. At the Vegetarian Festival in Thailand, however, you can enjoy a bowl of veggie noodles or curry (hard to find during the rest of the year), but the main event of this annual cleansing period is body piercing—and it's pretty extreme! Participants in the Gin Jay Festival channel evil spirits and mutilate themselves by stabbing their skin with gigantic sticks and spears, sticking them all the way through. When the spears come out, so the story goes, the spirits are gone.

La Tomatina

If you like your gross festivals to be pretty tame, try the tomato fight in Spain. *La Tomatina* takes place every year at the end of August in Buñol. The tomato battle is the climax to a week of street parties, parades, lots of food and wine, and even fireworks. When the fiesta is over, the guts of over 90,000 tomatoes are spilled around the city.

Anyone up for a Nice Game of Headless Goat?

Polo is a highly civilized game played in the U.K. and India, where players ride around on horses hitting balls with mallets, right? So civilized that it's even known as "The Sport of Kings." Well, not always. There's a version that's a little more gruesome. It's called *buzkashi* and, instead of a ball, it uses a headless goat. It's Afghanistan's official sport and is popular throughout Central Asia.

Putting the "Ick" in Trick or Treat— Ideas for a Grossophile Halloween

Here are some easy tricks for spooking your friends at your next Halloween party. Stick these objects in bowls, blindfold your willing victims, guide their hands into the bowls, and tell them what they're feeling.

- Cold spaghetti for brains
- Dried apricots for ears
- Banana peel for tongues

RECIPE FOR FAKE BLOOD

1 pint white corn syrup
¼ cup creamy peanut butter
¼ cup dishwashing soap
red and blue food coloring
a clean bottle

- Stir in cup corn syrup into the peanut butter.
- Pour in the soap and a full bottle of red food coloring.
- Add the remaining corn syrup. Add blue food coloring drops until you get the right color.
- Pour into a bottle and go find someone to stab (for pretend)!

Fright Night

You might not need to leave the house to get goo and guts galore on Halloween. According to the website Pumpkin Nook, the innards of the pumpkin are referred to as brains, guts, sinew, goop, goo, and pumpkin slime. Sounds pretty yicky to us.

Halloween High Jinks

Gummy worms? That's nothing. How about gummy snakes? Or while the guests at your Halloween party have their hands in a bowl of peeled grapes, bring out the eyes of terror gumballs! The sight alone will send shivers down their spines. And don't forget to get infested. Cockroach bites have a nice realistic crunch to them.

Jawbreaker Horror

Regular old lollipops are *so* last century. How about a scorpion sucker instead! Then again, you could always go for the sour candies called Toxic Waste (yes, you really can buy—and eat—both of these things). If you'd rather go for real and not just realistic, maybe you'd be more interested in chocolate-covered cockroaches or other **Mouthwatering Frights,** see pg. 18.

You really can't get much grosser than Gummy Boo Boos Candy Scabs. From the Candy Warehouse website:

"*You've skinned your elbow while crashing your bicycle getting extreme over a gnarly jump in your neighborhood. You cry to your mommy and she gently places a bandage over the bloody spot. Two days later, you peel back the bandage to reassess the damage. That same spot is now oozy in the middle and crusty at the edges! SO NASTY! You know you want to lick that puss spot...don't deny it...and now you can... with Candy Scabs!*"

THE
HORRORS
OF MODERN
SCIENCE

The only thing worse than the cruel and barbaric practices of ancient history are the cruel and barbaric practices of today.

Pokey-Man

Sticking dozens of tiny needles in someone's skin—including their face? Okay, that must be some primitive medicine like bloodletting (see *Let My Blood Go*, pg. 54), leech therapy, or ritual sacrifice. Wrong! It's just a day in the life of your friendly neighborhood acupuncturist. The customer is the one who willingly subjects himself or herself to repeated needle insertion. The practice comes from the Chinese tradition of alternative medicine. It doesn't actually hurt as much as it looks really disturbing. So keep your eyes shut!

Eyes Wide Open

When you get retinal eye surgery, the surgeon has to take out your entire eye bulb. We're guessing you're not awake while this happens. If you are, that would definitely be a sight for sore eyes—your own.

Did You Know? *Acupuncture began by accident when the ancient Chinese noticed that when arrow wounds didn't kill the victim, they often helped solve various ailments, including asthma. Pretty good proof that whatever doesn't kill you makes you stronger.*

3, 2, 1, Liftoff!

Astronauts have to wear a form of diapers. But on a rocketship, they go by a somewhat classier, more discreet name: Maximum Absorbency Garments. Yikes—anything with maximum absorption must be able to carry quite a load when full.

You Look a Little Pale

Blood-injection-injury phobia is classified by the DSM-IV (the *Diagnostic and Statistical Manual of Mental Disorders*). Experts believe it's a disorder learned through trauma. An elevated heart rate and/or fainting at the sight of blood or during a medical procedure are common. As we mentioned earlier, some people argue that it may have once been an adaptive trait that allowed members of a group who fainted during an attack to have been left for dead by the enemy and ended up surviving.

In Praise of Stinky Feet

The Bill and Melinda Gates Foundation provided a grant to recreate foot odor in mosquito traps as part of a malaria-prevention project. This works because mosquitoes are attracted to the smell of sweaty feet. Well, to each his own.

The Return of the Maggots

In 2005, a woman named Pam Mitchell had a minor cut that got infected. The infection got so bad that eventually her doctor recommended amputation. As a last resort, Ms. Mitchell tried maggots, desperate to avoid the chopping block. She received 600 on one foot and 400 on the other, all alive and wrapped up in bandages. We don't know how long she had to walk around as a maggot factory. But, most importantly, did it work? Reportedly, yes. And her doctor seemed to agree.

Did You Know? Maggot therapy works by "debridement"—peeling away dead tissue.

Superbugs Fighting...Superbugs

Another roach sighting; better call the exterminator! Maybe not. It turns out that cockroaches may have something we want—a chemical that is toxic to harmful bacteria. British researchers have located molecules that can kill E. coli as well as the bacteria that causes staph infections inside the brains of none other than the soon-to-be guests at your local roach motel. (Locusts contain this chemical, too, though for most of us they tend to be less local.)

Bedside Gamble

On average, 100,000 people die a year from hospital-related infections or medical mistakes.

Did You Know? Surgeons are used to patients arriving with severed limbs in a bag of ice. Sometimes they're useable. But other times the body parts can't be sewn on and are consigned to the trash bin. Don't worry, there's a special trash for this kind of debris.

Be an Expert! *It's not uncommon to replace a missing thumb with a patient's big toe. Wonder what the patient says the next time he or she feels particularly clumsy. "I'm all thumbs!" (Well, not anymore.)*

Lessons from a Rat

Smell and disgust are designed partially to prevent food poisoning. A rat that eats a substance that makes him sick won't eat that substance again. That's an example of a *conditioned taste aversion*, an area of study pioneered by psychologist Edwin Ray Guthrie, who established the Law of Contiguity. The law says that a stimulus gets associated with a certain response whether or not there was a causal relationship. The rat that gets sick after eating a piece of chocolate and never eats it again is exhibiting one-trial learning. This is compared with your uncle Bob who gets sick once again from that fourth helping of Christmas pudding, just like he does every year. No one-trial (or two-trial or three-trial) learning going on there. We don't need to bother comparing humans to dolphins to determine who's smarter. Our bet is we can safely set the bar a little bit lower.

Be an Expert! *Unlike blood pudding, Christmas pudding is a legitimate dessert, but it contains "suet", which is basically beef fat collected from deposits near the kidneys and loins of a cow.*

The Cure Will Kill You

The side effects of some medicines are enough to make you run screaming from the doctor's office. Here are just a few side effects commonly listed for widely advertised modern drugs:

• skin rashes
• blindness
• coughing up blood
• black hairy tongue (for more details on that unfortunate predicament, see *Furry Lingua*, pg. 194)
• amnesia
• internal bleeding
• loss of senses
• heart attack or stroke that leads to death

Keep in mind these are all just things the medication might *introduce*. They're not related to the original problem you were trying to eradicate by taking medicine in the first place.

🧠 IN THE KNOW

Eradicate: to get rid of

TO EACH HIS OWN

(DISGUSTING HABITS)

REALLY, KEEP THESE THINGS TO YOURSELF...PLEASE!

Illegal Beans

Pythagoras, namesake of your trusty Pythagorean Theorem, was a Greek mathematician and philosopher who lived in the 500s B.C. Sure, he contributed to number theory and influenced Plato, yadda yadda yadda, but more importantly, he put a prohibition on the eating of beans. No explanation has survived, but later philosophers speculated that the brilliant thinker worried that farts would interfere with mental well-being and a good night's sleep. Try using that argument the next time you hear your dad channeling Louis Armstrong under the table.

Unique Knickknack

People have all different tastes in jewelry: some people like charm bracelets, some like old-fashioned pearls, and then of course there are those who like to wear their jewelry... *alive!* In 2010, a woman's brooch was seized by U.S. Customs and Border Protection because it was a live beetle. (And the beetle itself was wearing jewels.) Apparently, the daring fashionista needed a live plant pest importation document in order to bring her brooch into the country.

A Pinot Noir, Please, and Step on It

Sounds like a joke your kid brother would tell, but this one's true. Wine used to be made from stomping on grapes with bare feet, a custom that appears to date back to ancient Rome. This tradition continued right up until a decade or so ago. Guess a stranger's piggy toes and a romantic dinner for two just didn't go that well together. Certain countries still do the grape-stomp dance, so you if you're lucky you'll still be able to get a taste of some random person's bare feet after all. (Let's hope they skipped the toe rings and kept toe lint to a minimum.)

Here, Little Roachie

New Yorkers are typically more scared of cockroaches than of getting mugged, but the widely despised insect is considered a delicacy in some countries. In others, they're kept in the house alive and well...on purpose. In Australia, for example, a lack of space in urban areas has led to an increase in cockroaches being considered a member of the family. The rhinoceros cockroach (also known as the giant borrowing cockroach) can live up to a decade and, according to pet-store owners, is one of the most popular breeds.

Rhino roaches are clean and safe for children. Some stores have taken to calling them "litter bugs" or "rain beetles" to give the world's heftiest roach a wider appeal.

> *"There is nothing per se that is yucky about cockroaches. The ick factor is all psychological. Cockroaches are nice, lovely, interesting animals."*
>
> BIOLOGIST DR. MARLENE ZUK
> Author of *Riddled with Life: Friendly Worms, Ladybug Sex and the Parasites That Make Us Who We Are*

Playing Dead

He's not actually a dead body; he just plays one on TV. Lots of people teach their dogs to play dead, but Chuck Lamb, aka "Dead Body Guy," taught himself, by taking self-portraits that looked as if he'd been killed in all different ways, including being smashed by the automatic garage door or bludgeoned at his desk. He then posts the gruesome photos to his blog. Mr. Lamb's life dream was to play a dead guy onscreen, and he finally made it, cast as a corpse in

The Book of the Dead and *Kentucky Horror Show* and landing an appearance in a body bag for the series *Stiffs*. In case there wasn't enough mutton lying around in their freezer, the Carnegie Deli hung a picture of Lamb in his favorite repose, an indisputable sign that Dead Body Guy's fantasies had finally come to life.

Barbaric Amulet

Some people carry a lucky rabbit's foot (not so lucky for the rabbit) on a keychain or in their pocket as a talisman to bring good fortune. The fur is often dyed a bright color. In North America, there are certain stipulations attached to the "lucky" foot, including that the rabbit was either found in a graveyard or shot, that it's a left foot, and that the foot must be cut off before the rabbit is killed. So, let's hop to it. Is this your lucky day? How about a nice four-leaf clover or horseshoe instead?

How Low Will You Go?

What would you do for a million dollars? Would you confront the things that terrify you? Shows like *Survivor*, *The Mole*, and especially *Fear Factor* have tested the outer limits of grossness tolerance. Some contestants swim in blood, some have buckets of cockroaches dumped on them, and others have to eat insects.

Give Me Cow Dung or Give Me Death—or Both

The Greek philosopher Heraclitus had a strange relationship to excrement. He thought that cow manure would help ease his edema. Acting on that belief, Heraclitus dunked himself in a nice hot tub of fresh cow droppings. We'll never know if it would have cured the swelling because the swollen wise man ended up meeting his end in that tub, drowning in cow dung. Have you ever heard the phrase "No man steps in the same river twice"? Maybe whoever first said it was thinking of poor Heraclitus. Once he stepped in, he never stepped out.

🧠 IN THE KNOW

Edema: a condition where fluid collects
and leads to swelling in various organs

HEINOUS HOBBIES

A man named Barney Smith keeps a collection of toilet seats alongside various other odd paraphernalia, including sets of false teeth and license plates. Hey, whatever floats your boat. (On second thought, a ship collection would be way too mainstream for this odd duck.) Still, this is all pretty tame compared to the couple that collected so much garbage in their house, they couldn't get out (see *Don't Keep Your Trash Heap*, pg. 59).

I See Your Guitar and Raise You One Eyebrow

Have you ever seen a one-man band? We'll bet you've never seen this variety—a man in Arkansas can play with bells attached to his eyebrows.

Barbaric Amulet

Some people carry a lucky rabbit's foot (not so lucky for the rabbit) on a keychain or in their pocket as a talisman to bring good fortune. The fur is often dyed a bright color. In North America, there are certain stipulations attached to the "lucky" foot, including that the rabbit was either found in a graveyard or shot, that it's a left foot, and that the foot must be cut off before the rabbit is killed. So, let's hop to it. Is this your lucky day? How about a nice four-leaf clover or horseshoe instead?

Gross Collections

When it comes to collections, forget boring old Matchbox cars, stamps, and coins. Get your mind in the gutter! How about trying out these ideas for a bit of boorish fun. These are real-life collections that people like to keep:
• Naval fluff (aka belly lint)
• Clipped fingernails
• Beard clippings
• Burned food

Divided Afterlife

The French Cardinal La Grange had an unusual post-mortem request: to bury his bones at Avignon and the rest of what was left at Amiens. It certainly gives a new meaning to "dividing up an estate".

Crying Milk

You know not to cry over spilled milk, but you may gag when you see Jim Chicon snort it out his eye! We don't know how he figured out that he could do it. Maybe he took his cue from the horny toad, who shoots something even worse out of his (see *Did You Know?* in Outlandish Animals).

Mean Machine

History buffs should think twice before making their own guillotine. In one instance, a fake model led to a very real disaster. A man in Washington lost his arm when he was cleaning his overly accurate facsimile. A nearby woman saw the man running around, gushing blood with a missing arm and said she hoped it was a Halloween costume. (By strange coincidence, the accidental chopping took place in October.) Sadly, it was not. Police found the arm left at the scene of the hacking.

CAREERS FOR GROSSOPHILES

Various jobs you might want to consider post-graduation, if you can stomach them:

- **Make-up artist for dead people**
- **Scatologist:** someone who studies ancient excrement
- **Forensic pathologist:** a doctor who conducts autopsies to determine the cause of death. From watching crime shows, you may know this role as a medical examiner, or M.E. (*Bonus:* You can vent endlessly to office mates about the stress of the job without fear of repercussion.)
- **Bad-breath evaluator.** *Really!* There are people who have to rate people's dragon breath in order to test various "fresh-breath" products.

What do you want to be when you grow up?

Well, if you're not afraid to get your hands dirty, break out the industrial-strength hand sanitizer. The Discovery Channel has a show called *Dirty Jobs*, a showcase for those brave workers doing the jobs no one else wants to do, including sewer inspector, fish factory worker, worm dung farmer, roadkill cleaner, owl vomit collector, and maggot farmer.

Bring in the Horns

Pythagoras (See *Illegal Beans*, pg. 92) would have surely debated him, but Roman Emperor Claudius would be a welcome addition to your junior-high lunchroom. The windy ruler created a law allowing farting at banquets on the grounds that retaining gas could be harmful to your health.

One Bag the Airlines Still Aren't Charging for

There is an online museum dedicated to airsickness bags. People who donate bags to the museum's collection are identified as "Patrons of Puke." Let's hope none of the bags are used.

Animal Friendly

One original thinker has an unusual take on the omnivore's dilemma–he eats only animals that have been killed accidentally. Whether it's a rat, dog, badger, or bat, there's always room on Arthur Boyle's plate for roadkill, preferably fresh. (Wonder if he draws the line at hominoids...)

Reappearing Mice

If you or a friend has ever had a pet snake, you may have seen frozen mice in the freezer, ready for mealtime. That wily snake can swallow them whole. Big deal, right? But did you know some people can swallow them whole, too? (Why they would want to is another question all together.) One Jewish German circus performer named Waldo, known as the "Regurgitating Geek" could not only swallow a mouse whole but, you guessed it, regurgitate it back up alive and well. He trained himself to do the same with fish, frogs, and even rats. If anyone ever asks you to join their regurgitating act, just say yuck!

Bearded Man

An eye-catching beard is often the only recourse to distract from male-pattern balding. See, *I do have hair, just not on my head!* But Edwin Smith, a 19th-century gold-rush miner, had hair just about everywhere. At its peak (and we don't mean widow's), his beard alone was 8 feet long. Rubbing it like a philosopher must have given him an awful lot of time to think.

Don't Be so Sensitive

In the book *The Big Book of Gross Stuff* by Bart King, there is a woman whose skin is so reactive, she can draw pictures on it. She then sells the photographs she takes of the drawings she scratches into her skin, and apparently people hang them up on their wall as art. Guess art really is in the eye of the beholder (or, in this case, the skin of the maker).

"Best by" Date is a Personal Opinion

Think you're fearless because you willingly eat foods that have passed their expiration date? In a study, 64 percent of women say they've done it. (We're guessing men do it all the time, either without realizing or admitting to it.) Guess you weren't quite as adventurous as you thought the last time you chugged down that O.J. from last winter. Maybe it's time to start dusting off that hang glider instead.

Useful Poop

Why waste a good patch of marsupial poop? In Australia, a company makes roo poo paper out of it.

Flinging Feces

If your principal gives you a suspension for misbehavior, count your blessings. A Canadian principal once threw poop at a problematic student. Um, that is just *so* not okay. (The principal got a suspension—a long one, called "an absolute discharge"—kind of like what she threw?—but last we heard, she was being officially pardoned.

Don't Stop 'Til You Drop (Dead)

Some nicotine addicts forced to breathe through a stoma have opted to smoke cigarettes through it instead.

 IN THE KNOW

Stoma: an opening in the neck made for patients to breathe through during throat cancer surgery.

Look Me up When I'm Gone

Mydeathspace.com is a real site where you can find up-to-the minute news on people who died. The main gimmick is that the site syncs up the obits with social media profiles. Outpourings of grief and messages to the dead are stored in their pages as ongoing interactive memorials.

 IN THE KNOW

Obits: (abbrev. for obituary) a brief article about someone who recently died; a death notice

Stretch that Neck

If you don't know what it is, rubbernecking sounds kind of gross all on its own. But it actually means craning your neck to see the wreckage of a car accident or some other gruesome sight. With their heads turned to the side, the gore gawkers tend to slow down their cars, so the traffic piles up not because of the accident itself, but because of the viewers intent on taking in the grisly scene.

Bon Voyage!

Here's an unusual gift idea for that hard-to-please person on your Christmas list—a cruise on a private yacht out to sea (after he or she has died). If the person is taking the final voyage unattended (by family and friends), it'll only set you back $150 at California company Burials at Sea, and they'll even throw in a video or photographs for those who stay behind. For a little more money, the deceased can take along a party of 12 on that final voyage. After the drop-off, they'll get to visit an island off the coast of L.A. to catch the sunset before the return cruise (for everyone but the guest of honor, that is).

UNNATURAL WONDERS

Step right up and take a whiff of flowers that smell like dead bodies, learn the truth about honey (it's vomit), and take a bite out of edible utensils. It's all part of the freak show in the perverse circus of oddities and grossology. You'll wish you couldn't believe your eyes...

Is that a Rigor Mortis I Smell?

Ahhh, nothing like the beautiful smell of fresh flowers to cheer you up—unless, of course, you're sticking your whiffer into a corpse flower, which really does have the odor of a dead body. The name alone should give you a hint to steer clear, unless you only hear it called by its official designation: *Amorphophallus titanium*. If you know Greek, you might guess that means "giant misshapen penis," and you'd be right. The smell for sore noses was later renamed *titan arum*, which sounded a bit more proper. The next time you smell a dead body, it's more likely a real one than a plant that smells like one, since the corpse flower by any name is a finicky plant that's tricky to grow; you're not all that likely to run into one.

Decorative Geckos

If you found a bug or spider in your hotel room, you might not be pleased, but presumably you wouldn't freak out, either. But how about a gecko? Or maybe you're not sure what a gecko is. A gecko is a small chirping lizard that lives in warm climates and can climb walls and even ceilings, thanks to tiny suction cups built into its feet. These suckers

are commonplace in certain countries, like Madagascar and Brazil, and can be found in warm regions of the United States. And watch out—nocturnal and known to let go without warning. Free-falling geckos at midnight! They are, however, harmless and eat pests such as mosquitoes. So if one lands on your head just as you're nodding off, remember things could be worse. (See *Home Away from Home*, pg. 135.)

It's Not the Bee's Knees

You might be disgusted by the level of insect carcasses that the FDA tolerates in food, but did you ever stop to think that honey comes out of a bee's stomach? Yes, that delicious syrup you pour in your tea is technically vomit.

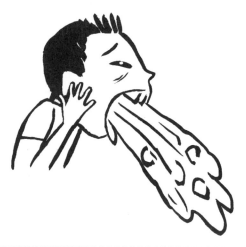

Skunk Cabbage (Symplocarpus foetidus)

In the swamplands of eastern North America, you'll find the putrid-smelling plant that got its name from the striped omnivore famous for its pungent spray. Can you believe its pollinators are actually *attracted* to the smell of the skunk cabbage? It does make sense, however, when you think of the party insects throw when you leave out a piece of rotting fruit. We eat *regular* cabbage but what about the stinky kind? Parts of the root and early leaves *are* edible for humans, but they need to be dried out thoroughly and then cooked. All of which probably falls into the "don't try this at home" category.

IN THE KNOW

Omnivore: an animal that eat both plants and animals

IN THE KNOW

Pollinators: the insects that help with fertilization by spreading pollen from a flower's male parts to its female parts

Feeling Prickly

Beware of barberry bushes—they're awfully prickly, as Jens Jensen can tell you. He fell into one once and came out with a few thorns—exactly 32,131. Glad we didn't have to help him pull those out.

Jurassic Retch

Vomit is biodegradable, so it doesn't usually stick around for long. But in one case, it stuck around for a little while—160 million years, to be (sort of) exact. In 2002, English paleontologists found fossilized dinosaur vomit. ("Fossilized Dinosaur Vomit"—there's a good gross band name for you to add to the list! See *Farts & Culture*, pg. 217!)

Be an Expert! *The fossilized vomit found by paleontologists was full of a kind of shellfish called belemnites.*

I'm so Hungry, I Could Eat a Fork

Why stop at eating the food *on* your utensils? Why not make a clean sweep of it and eat the utensils themselves? At a university in the Midwest, a group of students came up with the idea of turning oats into edible utensils for an Entrepreneurship Immersion program. They call the products "Greenolies," and they won $4,500 for the innovation.

It's Gettin' Hot in the Barnyard

Greenhouse gases are a major threat to life on Earth. We all know cars and factories are major polluters, but did you know that Old Bessie is doing her share of releasing methane into the atmosphere? And not by excessive flatulence, as is commonly thought. Every year, gassy bovines belch out 100 million tons of hydrocarbons.

THE INDECENT TOURIST

We know you were too embarrassed to ask your French exchange student, but yes, it's true that in France and other parts of Europe they have bidets—little bathtubs to wash their private parts. In some parts of the world, it's okay to burp during a meal. Certain tribes in South America keep dead relatives in their attic. People really do eat scorpions, earthworms, grasshoppers, jellyfish, and even cockroaches (for more on this, see *Bizarre Cuisine*). If nothing else, traveling around the world will get you outside your comfort zone. In some cases, light years away.

Pig Everlasting

The world's oldest tree, longest-living dog, or most ancient dinosaur fossil...these all seem like fairly honorable distinctions. But world's oldest ham? Yes, indeed. This celebrated hind leg is on display at the Isle of Wight County Museum in the U.K. The gammon was cured in 1902, set aside, forgotten about for 20 years, then rediscovered and taken on tour as a famous "pet" ham. It's still going strong today. That swine sure has staying power!

Bottom's up, Literally

The Yanomami of South America say, "Bottom's up" in memory of dead relatives by drinking a cocktail of banana juice mixed with their ashes. The hope is that the good attributes of the deceased will pass on to the living.

Did You Know? Frozen-meat stocked vending machines are commonplace in Tokyo, Japan. "Hmmm, do I feel like potato chips, cookies, or roast beef today?"

And You Thought Foot and Mouth Disease Was Bad

We've all heard of people fighting animals for fun. At least the Saxons who fought horses to death had the decency to do it in the Dark Ages. In Spain, bullfights are quite popular, even today. The third act of the fight is called the *tercio de meurte* (the "death third"), so it's no surprise that the gruesome spectacle ends up with one party getting killed—almost always the bull. In the summer of 2010, a bull took revenge on Julio Aparacio (who'd killed hundreds of his relatives) by impaling the matador with his horn. It went directly through Aparacio's neck and out his mouth. The craziest part is: the matador survived! (We're not sure about the bull. If he did, too, it probably wasn't for long.)

Bittersweet

Honey isn't always sweet. In his *Travels in the Interior of Brazil* written in the mid-19th century, Scottish botanist George Gardner reports on the 18 different types of honey he came upon, all offered by indigenous people. The Borá honey is described as "acid." The Mumbúco after an hour "becomes as sour as lemon juice," and from the Oarití is "blackish...sour, and not good." When you call someone "sweet as honey," make sure you're a good distance away from the Amazon River.

Just a Pinch of Salt

Do you remember the scene in the TV show *Seinfeld* where Kramer bastes himself in the hot tub after accidentally cooking himself with butter? You, too, can take part in your own soup! Just hop into a garlic-flavored spa bath in Hakone, Japan. You'll never worry about garlic breath again after a garlic bath leaves your entire body reeking of the stuff.

The Eggs Won't Be Sunny Side up

You won't go home hungry after a Bedouin wedding. The main course alone will hold you if you can hold *it*. It's a camel stuffed with sheep stuffed with chickens stuffed with fish stuffed with eggs (one inside the other, kind of like those Russian nesting dolls).

The Body in the Attic

In the West, it's not uncommon to cremate someone and keep their ashes on the mantelpiece. The Murats of North Borneo in East Malaysia have an interesting practice for honoring their dead. They fold dead bodies of relatives into jars and store them on their roofs, drawing liquid off through a bamboo pipe. After a year, they bury the bones, which is all that's left by that point.

You Don't Have a Leg to Stand on

Someone once left a stuffed crocodile behind in their hotel room. Kind of hard to forget, don't you think? Hmm, then again, maybe it's not as odd as forgetting a prosthetic leg, which, according to hotel proprietors, is quite common. Finding a spare body part must be an unsettling experience for the person who happens upon it, but even stranger for the person who left it behind. "I feel like I'm missing something?" Hop, hop, hop.

Thank You—Burp—Very Much

Junior-high kids the world over will be thrilled to know that it's sometimes polite to burp at the dinner table. In Japan, it can be a sign that you appreciate the meal. Certain Bedouin tribes are also fond of a respectful belch. So don't be afraid to slurp and burp.

Paris Down Under

When in Paris, don't miss the Louvre, Notre Dame, or the Eiffel Tower. And last but not least, the *pièce de résistance*: a tour of the sewers. They have their own dedicated museum, *Le Musée des Égouts de Paris*. Don't get lost in there.

IN THE KNOW

Pièce de résistance: the most important item; the showpiece

Be an Expert! *The sewers under Paris play a role in both* Les Misérables *and* Phantom of the Opera.

You've Got All the Time in the World

A native tribe in Malaysia takes the expression "no rush" to a whole new level. They wait two decades after a person dies before burying the body.

Slippery Divers

Scuba diving is a popular honeymoon activity for thrill-seekers, but some people took the romance out of deep-sea diving by purposely diving under the gulf oil spill in 2010.

🧠 IN THE KNOW

Papadum: a spiced wafer common in India

Did You Know? In India, kissing in public is considered gross. So keep PDA (public displays of affection) to a minimum while chowing down on your papadum.

When in China

In China, it is considered coarse to finish everything on your plate. The host may take that to mean that you are still hungry. So, gobble up the all-you-can-eat dumplings, but leave a little *dan dan mein* for the patron saint of good manners.

Hop on in

Many cultures consider a frog a mouthwatering item. In Peru and Bolivia, you'll even find them leaping into juices and smoothies. When you stop to think about it, "all-natural" ingredients casts a rather wide net.

"What a Big Mouth You Have!" "The Better to Taste You with, My Dear."

In Oegstgeest, Holland you can climb inside a giant mouth in a human body museum. Is that an earthquake? No, it's just the realistic soundtrack, complete with the sounds of digestion.

Human Body—It Does a Body Good!

The Aztecs had a signature dish with corn and unusual ingredient—man! But don't heave, plenty of members of the animal kingdom would be happy to have vomit for lunch. (See *Lose Your Lunch on Purpose*, pg. 14.)

Messy Tapas

When in Spain, let the crumbs rain down (along with napkins and any other trash). The restaurant picks it up and does not expect the patrons to help in any way. (After all, you're probably still tired. It may only have been an hour or so since your last siesta!)

Be an Expert! "Que asco" *means "How gross" in Spanish.*

Scorpion Stickup

When in Beijing, don't forget to try a skewered scorpion. They may be toxic little creatures when they're alive, but not when served up on a stick. (If you're worried, see *Score for Scorpion Lovers*, pg. 31.)

Be an Expert! You can also sample snake skin and silkworms while touring the capital of China.

Did You Know? Scorpions are found on every continent but Antarctica.

CREEPY CRAWLIES

From the world's biggest wasp to bloodsuckers that target your mouth while you sleep, this is the stuff of which horror movies are made.

Whole Lotta Bugs

 Maybe you're a naturalist who has been a bug fan your whole life, hunting fireflies in the summer, keeping caterpillars through the winter, and stalking roly-polies in the spring. Think you've seen, or at least heard, about most bugs? Think again. There are 900,000 unique species of insects on Earth. If you compare the number of different kinds of insects to other species and charted it on a pizza pie, about 6½ slices would be bugs; the remaining slice and a half would be everything else. Anyone feel like ordering a pizza? While you're eating, take a guess at just how many ACTUAL bugs there are crawling around our planet right now.

Be an Expert! *Roly-polies are officially known as* Armadillidiidae, *but they're also called pillbugs or potato bugs. They're not actually insects; they're* crustaceans. *And they really can roll up quite neatly into a ball.* Cool! *But they also eat poop.* Yuck.

Planet of the Roaches

You may have heard that cockroaches landed on the planet before we did, but did you know that they lived it up for a good 200 million years before the earliest humans? These nasty insects are extremely adaptable when it comes to surviving in all but the most extreme conditions (some species have even lasted more than four weeks without eating), so they're likely to be the last bug standing should another great wave of extinctions occur. They're resourceful when they lose body parts (see *Headless Roachman*, pg. 177). Plus, they can move along at a brisk pace of 3 miles an hour, which means, if they could sustain it, they'd easily keep up with you on a stroll through the park. Lucky for us, they scurry out of sight when bigger creatures enter a room or turn on a light. (At least most of them—flying cockroaches are another story all together.)

Hostess with the Mostess

There is a kind of parasitic wasp that's quite efficient at finding a home for its eggs. They simply make a hole inside the eggs of a beetle and lay the eggs right there in their host. Talk about overstaying your welcome!

Poison Alehouse

A pub in Southampton, Hampshire, in England, was the unsuspecting home to what the *Daily Mail* called a "record-breaking infestation"—a gigantic wasp nest 6 feet by 5 feet, with 500,000 stingers inside. Bet drinks were on the house the night the bartender stumbled upon that load of venom. As their neighbors to the west might say when raising a toast, May the road rise up to meet you so you can get the hell out of that bar!

Android Ant

You may not be a huge ant fan, but it's still kind of too bad that there's a kind of fungi that can literally get inside their brains and turn them into zombies.

Queen-Size Bed

The termite queen is a productive leader, laying up to 8,000 eggs a day. The gelatinous creature can live up to half a century, even though she can't move. (Her tiny legs can't carry the weight of her enormous, goopy body.)

Leftover Lunch

When your parents remind you that spiders get rid of flies and other pests, you may agree to let the arthropod go on its merry way under the couch or behind the curtain. Still, it would be nice if they cleaned up after themselves instead of leaving ant carcasses all around the house.

Did You Know? In *2011, Arizona State University hosted an Ugly Bug Contest with a western theme. The Seed Beetle took first prize. The Flower Beetle (a misleading name, we're guessing?) was a close second.*

Mellow Yellow

Have you ever seen the yellow residue left by ladybugs, maybe on your finger after you've been holding one? It's blood. The colorful critters release it as a defense mechanism. The smell keeps predators away.

All the Bugs You Can Eat

Spiders each gulp down about 2,000 pesky insects a year. Flies are a favorite meal, but some eat really big stuff. Tarantulas, for example, eat mice. Good to know if you're planning to keep either one as a pet.

> **Did You Know?** *A fishing spider feeds on small fish. We'd like to see that! Actually, we wouldn't. But it sounds riveting in a nauseating way. These spiders don't make webs to trap their prey, but they do make webs — for their young. Because of the care they take doing that, they're also somewhat affectionately known as nursery web spiders.*

Home Away from Home

"Don't let the bedbugs bite" used to be a cute little rhyme for tucking toddlers in bed at night. Like "See you later, alligator", the speaker didn't actually mean to allude to the potential threat of any invasive or dangerous creature lurking around. But, bedbug infestations have exploded in recent years. Paranoid travelers will want to inspect their hotel rooms for bed bugs before unpacking their stuff. Use a flashlight and peer under the mattress, looking around the seams in

Be an Expert! Like mosquitoes, bedbugs feed on the blood of humans. They're a pain in the neck (and other parts of the body), but fortunately, they're not known to spread disease.

particular and any other places the critters could hide. Besides live bugs, the Environmental Protection Agency says to search for: bedbug poop, red stains, tiny white eggs and shells, and skins (apparently they shed at some point in their life cycle).

The Bug Club

If creepy crawlies don't bug you...then the Bug Club might be just the thing for you. Find the "Amateur Entomologist's Society" online to join. Learn about the life cycles, body parts, and classification of your favorite bugs. And if your parents are still holding out on allowing a dog, cat, or even a gerbil, maybe you can sell them on a smaller pet with a few more feet (or none at all). On the Bug Club site, you'll find care sheets for everything from caterpillars to scorpions to cockroaches. For more ideas on what to get, see *World's Grossest Pets*, pg. 183.

Be an Expert! Your pet tarantulas will be grateful for a snack of crickets and locusts. A giant millipede can be fed with compost made from kitchen scraps.

Great Balls of Fire!

Here's more compelling proof that you don't have to go further than nature to find stuff crazier than the most outrageous science fiction. During the honeybee mating ritual, the male genitalia explodes inside the female.

Did You Know? *If you are feeding a spider live food, make sure to remove the food when it's not mealtime. Otherwise the meal itself could turn the tables.*

Shake-a-Leg (or 1,000)

Centipedes and millipedes are both arthropods. They look like worms, but they're more like insects or crustaceans—though not the kind we'd like to shake hands with, even just one. Some millipedes release cyanide!

Be an Expert! Identify a millipede by the double pair of legs attached to each segment of its body (centipedes have only one pair per segment).

The New Beatles

Slime-mold beetles—the name alone catapults them into the realm of the extremely disgusting. When a batch of new species of these slimy-moldy insects was discovered, the entomologists in charge of their classification decided to honor George Bush, Dick Cheney, and Donald Rumsfeld with the new names for three of the critters: *Agathidium bushi* Miller and Wheeler, *Agathidium cheneyi* Miller and Wheeler and *Agathidium rumsfeldi* Miller and Wheeler. There's some esoteric trivia for you!

IN THE KNOW

Esoteric: understood only by experts or those with a specialized knowledge base

Off with His Head

Insect reproduction may be unpleasant enough on its own, but in case it's too run-of-the-mill for your taste, why not throw a little cannibalism in there, just for good measure? The male praying mantis better get down on his knees and pray for mercy during courtship. In captivity at least, the female is known to bite off her partner's head after reproduction.

Feces, It's What's for Dinner

When a fly decides to join your picnic, you really don't know where it's been before joining you. But flies aren't the only ones who partake of gross things like poop on purpose. According to Brenna Lorenz's popular website The Scoop on Poop, lots of organisms opt for fecal matter when it comes time to sit down to dinner: gorillas, dogs, and rabbits among them.

Spit it out

Yellow jackets and horne's make their nests by mixing their saliva with pieces of wood fibers and bark. They really put themselves into their work.

Out, Out, Damn Tick

Ticks carry a wide range of blood-borne bacteria. If you find one on your skin, use tweezers to remove it. Try to grab it near the mouth rather than near the stomach. Pull straight to avoid breaking off pieces of the tick, which may then be harder to remove. Many people recommend saving the tick to show your doctor if need be, though most ticks are harmless. The kind that carries Lyme disease is, unfortunately, the tiniest—the size of a sesame seed—and extremely hard to spot.

Roses Are Red, and so Are Some Bugs

If you're in the habit of reading the list of ingredients of the foods you consume or the makeup you wear, maybe you've heard of cochineal, carmine, or carminic acid. They sound harmlessly vague enough. Carmine is another word for a strong red color, like crimson, and also goes by the name natural red #4. All that seems okay. The problem is, these ingredients all come from the same thing—cochineals, which are—*wait for it*—insects! The beetlelike critters are found in Central and South America, crushed up, and then boiled to get the carminic acid that, once treated with alum, gives off that lovely red hue found in everything from blush to yogurt to ruby red grapefruit juice (or should we say grubby red?). On the plus side, beetles have a lot of protein.

Did You Know? You may be an entomophagist (someone who eats bugs, not to be confused with an entomologist, someone who studies them) and not even know it!

Four Eyes x 2

The fact that many spiders have eight legs is no big deal. What's weird is that many have the same number of eyes! So if you see one crawling across your wall, you can be sure it laid eyes on your first.

Hording Together

One or two locusts alone are fine. It's the "swarm" that gets a little off-putting. Scientists are starting to understand what makes locusts—otherwise solitary creatures—band together into a flock. It may be related to the sudden swelling of a neurochemical we have in common, called serotonin. That happens during famine and may help the species survive by grouping together into what's known as a "gregarious phase." Is this the same phenomenon that accounts for the swarm of hungry dinner guests at a wedding buffet?

Did You Know? Forget climbing up the water spout. Some kinds of wolf spiders can actually walk on water.

> **Did You Know?** *A camel spider is not a spider; it's a solpugid, also known as a wind scorpion. The nocturnal creatures aren't poisonous, but they're big (6 inches long) and can run faster that most of us, at 10 miles per hour. They're also especially creepy because they often run behind people (but only because they want to stay in your shadow, out of the light).*

Kissing Bug

Judging from the name kissing bug, it sounds like it must be something gentle and sweet like a ladybug or a butterfly, right? Far from it. Turns out it's a bloodsucker that zeroes in on your mouth and eyes while you sleep.

Et Tu, Brutal Bug?

Assassin bug—the name alone will give you nightmares. And it's apropos. The assassin bug stakes out a hiding spot from which to ambush its prey. Its sticky legs help then hold the victim while it is poisoned and then sucked from the inside out.

ICKY HISTORY

Phlegm, blood, yellow bile, and black bile—these are the four components the ancient Greeks believed made up the human body. They called them "humors". That word didn't mean the same thing it means to us, but those ancient wise guys were on to something. They must have known that a couple millenniums later, spit, blood, barf, and crap would end up being the butt of many, many jokes.

Lose Your Lunch on Purpose

Oh, there's nothing like piling your plate high at Thanksgiving with turkey, stuffing, mashed potatoes, cranberry sauce, and yams. Ever wish you weren't so stuffed so you could dive in for round two? The ancient Romans had a solution—though not a very tidy one. They used to make themselves vomit so they could eat more. Not much of a palette cleanser! At least they had the decency to start again with new food, not like cats, which are known for reconsuming what they just upchucked. And, of course, there are the bird moms that feed their little ones a homemade puree of regurgitated food. Wolves are fans of repeats, too. (See *The Last Supper, as in, the One You Just Had*, pg. 152.)

> *Did You Know?* Ancient Romans used pee to wash their clothes. (No, and maybe you didn' t want to know...)

Feeling Torn

Female prisoners of the Thuringians, a German tribe, met an unlucky end. Each arm was tied around a different horse's neck. Then the horses took off in opposite directions, and the victims got torn apart. In other documented cases of icky history, it was the horses themselves that received the bitter ending.

Call of the Wild Bluff

The remains of more than 100,000 unlucky bovines were found in a heap at the bottom of a cliff in what's now France. Historians believe that ancient humans had developed a

Did You Know? President Theodore Roosevelt once watched piranhas devour a cow down to its bones. In his book Through the Brazilian Wilderness, *he paints a colorful picture of what he calls "the most ferocious fish in the world" and the "rabid, furious snaps of its teeth".*

simple way to kill horses—chase them off an overhang and let them die by hitting the ground below. Hope no one was out for a quiet stroll below the cliffs.

Bender Contenders

It was hard to tell if F. Velez Campos was coming or going at any given time. Campos was a contortionist who could bend his knees in either direction. Another flexible fellow was Martin Joe Laurello, who could spin his head 180 degrees. These guys would have made terrific gang members in movies. The chase scenes alone would be enough to earn their keep.

Did You Know? *A woman once had a 37-foot tapeworm removed from her stomach. How did it get there? She must have consumed an infected piece of meat that was not thoroughly cooked. Better to err on the safe side: order meat well done rather than rare.*

If You Build It, They Will Come...
Unless They're Already Dead and You're
Building It with Their Skeletons

We've got a recommendation for a new stop on your next grisly European tour....Outside Prague, in the Czech Republic, there's a skeleton cathedral featuring chalices, crosses, and columns—all made of human bones. When dead bodies piled up due to a plague and various wars, mass graves overflowed. Rather than trying to find a new place to store them, church leaders put them to good use in the building of the church.

Did You Know? In crowded cities, it's hard enough to find enough room for people to live in, let alone die. There were traditionally cemeteries adjacent to the church, but after a plague or two, those things were packed to the rafters. This gave rise to the suburban garden cemetery, where Victorians liked to picnic and spend a leisurely Sunday afternoon.

Everybody Multitasks

We all agree that the presidential office should be treated with dignity and respect. It might be a little hard to refrain from junior-high humor, though, if the president insists on meetings while he's on the john. Supposedly Lyndon B. Johnson was a fan of just this kind of multitasking, as staff members were instructed to stand outside the door. (We're glad they weren't invited in! That would take it one step too far.)

Anything for Beauty, Literally

Maria Callas was said to have intentionally eaten a tapeworm to assist with her diet. Besides the gross factor of having a tapeworm in your tummy, there are some rather unpleasant side effects, including diarrhea, anemia, and liver disease. We'd recommend diet and exercise instead.

Look out Below!

"Bathroom language" is something we try to avoid in polite company. But once upon a time, there were no bathrooms to speak of. People simply went in pots and dumped it out the window, sending a warning to passersby below. (Don't worry, the waste eventually made its way to the sewer.)

Ghastly Extraction

In the 1800s, surgeons used a "tonsil guillotine" to remove tonsils. They were generally pretty adept at dislodging the lymphoid tissue, but often gave their patients a royal case of hemorrhaging at the same time.

Let my Blood Go

Bloodletting: the ancient medical practice, a description of which is generally followed by the "Aren't you glad you're alive now?" rhetorical question. Bloodletting was the practice of deliberately drawing blood from a patient in the hopes that it would heal him or her and was used to treat a wide range of maladies. It was recommended as late as 1923. We're trying to imagine the conversation in the operating room:

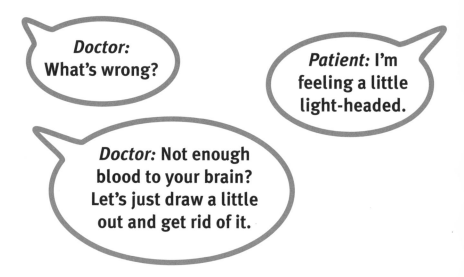

Doctor: What's wrong?

Patient: I'm feeling a little light-headed.

Doctor: Not enough blood to your brain? Let's just draw a little out and get rid of it.

Look out—we hear bloodletting is making a comeback.

Man's Best Friend to the End

In Medieval times, the brains of dogs were routinely used to dress wounds. Your guess is a good as ours!

For Those about to Die, We Apologize

Gladiators were real. In those progressive Roman times that gave rise to so much philosophical wisdom and mathematical breakthroughs, gladiators were slaves who fought to the death for the pleasure of their masters. And it wasn't just a few sadistic, twisted emperors who enjoyed watching humans die a bloody death: 50,000 spectators eagerly cheered along at the fights that had begun as funeral rites.

IN THE KNOW

Sadistic: the quality of enjoying watching others suffer

Did You Know? Fertility drugs go way back. In ancient Rome, a good cup of gladiator blood was sure to increase your chances of conception. So there was a silver lining to the dead gladiator's abandoned armor: the fight to the death gave birth to new life.

A Spoonful of Poison Helps the Medicine Go Down

When you get sick, your parents may bring you herbal tea or hot chocolate and, if you need it, medicine that tastes like grape or cherry. Here are some cures of days past that, in our opinion, would only have made you sicker!

- Garlic-fried cockroaches for indigestion (1800s)
- Maggots used to clean wounds (shockingly, this is still done. See *The Return of the Maggots*, pg. 85)
- Mice sake (in China today)
- Mercury for syphilis (now known to be extremely toxic)
- Earthworm soup (in China, to reduce fever)

Be glad you were born when you were. On second thought, maybe it's still just as bad. (See *The Cure Will Kill You*, pg. 89)

Pay for Pee, Pal

The Roman Emperor Nero taxed pee—and now we fine people who pee in public (otherwise known as taxation for presentation). On the other end of the scale, restroom users in fancy restaurants and clubs have to pay to pee. Or at least provide a tip (afterward, when someone hands them a towel).

Raining Rats and Dogs

Watching terrier dogs tear apart rats is a bizarre sport. In the 19th century, Europeans flocked to the pub to watch canines devour rodents in the pit.

No Pain, No Gain

Be glad you live in the time of anesthetic. In times past, often all you were given during an operation was a bit of brandy and a wood chip. How did the wood chip work? Well, instead of screaming, you just chomped down as hard as you could. Yowsers!!

Voodoo Catch-22

You might want to keep that Wicca book well hidden if you come across a time machine and find yourself growing up in 17th-century Salem, Massachusetts. Suspected witches were thrown in the ocean. If you drowned, that meant you were innocent. If you floated, that meant you were guilty— and put to death. Talk about damned if you do, damned if you don't!

Friends Don't Let Friends Shrink Each Other's Heads

Head shrinking was a real thing. After killing an enemy, you chopped off their head, took out the brains, boiled the rest, and let it hang out to dry into this nice, neat little pinhead, the hair still intact.

Double-Cross Eyes

Talk about double vision—there was once a Chinese emperor with two pupils, in each eye! When he told a guest he'd like to see him again sometime, he wasn't kidding. We wonder if he ever adapted Humphrey Bogart's famous toast from the movie *Casablanca*. "Here's looking at you, kid... And make it a double."

Did You Know? Stonewall Jackson's left arm received a formal military funeral. (But we want to know: What happened to the rest of him?)

Foot Bone Connected to the...
Machine that Causes Cancer?

Up until recently, you could walk into a shoe store and stick your foot into an X-ray machine to check out the foot bones. Ask your grandparents about it. The little Main Street novelty went the way of the jelly shoe, when it was discovered that these machines emitted radiation. As late as 1981, the cancer-causing fluoroscope was in use in a store in West Virginia. Upon being alerted to the danger (and the fact that by then it was illegal), the store put their best foot forward and got rid of it.

IN THE KNOW

Jelly shoe: ask your parents about these. Made of PVC plastic, they hit the fashion scene in 1982 (at the World's Fair in Knoxville, Tennessee) and was all the rage in the 1980s, along with neon colors, layered socks, shoulder pads, and the leg bandana. Hmm...this is giving us an idea for a *Gross-o-pedia* spin-off.

Did You Know? Ancient Egyptians used crocodile poop for birth control!

Just a Little Trim—of My Hair!

After *Sweeney Todd: The Demon Barber of Fleet Street,* you may have thought that you'd heard everything there is to know about butchering barbers. However, in medieval times barbers carried out many surgical procedures, often with little or no training. You could get your haircut and then get your gaping wound taped up.

A Brave Shave

You know those peppermint-striped poles in front of the local barbershop on Main Street? Those are old-fashioned and rather charming, aren't they? Ummm, not if you know what they stand for. The peppermint pole is symbolic. Since back in the days of barber butchers—I mean, surgeons— your coiffeur might also be the one drawing blood. As such, red stood for blood, white stood for the tourniquet, and the pole itself symbolized the stick gripped by the patient to make the vein protrude to make the procedure easier.

Hang in There

Historians believe that Jesus Christ was nailed at his wrists rather than through the palm of his hands, as depicted in standard images of Jesus on the cross. If he'd been nailed in his palms, the nail would have cut through his body and he would have fallen off the cross.

I'll Trade You One Dump...

Until the middle of the last century, human excrement was considered so valuable as fertilizer in Japan that it was often traded for eggplants and radishes.

"You're a Leech."
"Thank You."

Leech therapy may have started as early as 3,500 years ago. Given how many maladies they were used to address, we don't know why "leech" became such a negative word.

You Are What You Eat

A fourth-century Chinese alchemist recommended eating gold—if you could get your hands on it—to attain purification.

Lend Me a Hand—for Good

Thankfully, humans are law-abiding creatures. The oldest known extant laws were drawn up by Hammurabi of Babylon around 1700 B.C. and called Hammurabi's Code. A lot of the text seems quite reasonable, such as not blaming the victim, and so on. But certain parts are a little unnerving—for example, if a son hit his father, his hand would be lopped off. Not exactly a punishment that fits the crime, in our book.

Puke Cuke

King Sennacherib from ancient Assyria had some rather unusual bragging rights. About his enemies, he said: "I tore out their private parts like the seeds of cucumbers."

"To Life!" (Just Not the One of the Guy Whose Skeleton I'm Holding)

Before the Romans converted them into man-made cups, the Gauls used human skulls to glug delicious mead. Bottoms—or in this case, heads—up!

You Look Good Enough to Eat!

Some scientists believe that all humans are descendants of cannibals, although the Catholic Church has never been fond of the idea. Instead, it prefers virtual cannibalism in the form of the Eucharist: eating a wafer and sipping wine to represent eating the body of Christ and drinking his blood. Apparently, Christ himself directed his followers to eat him, saying, "This is my body" and "This is my blood." We always wondered what was on the menu for the Last Supper.

BOILS, FROGS, AND RIVERS OF BLOOD—OH MY!

When talking about gross stuff in history, why go back only as far as people burping and throwing up in the Middle Ages? There was tons of nightmarishly gross stuff going on before that. Who can forget the original top ten gross list in the Old Testament's Book of *Exodus*? Remember how the Hebrews were slaves in Egypt and wanted to leave, but Pharaoh wouldn't let them? Well, God went buck wild and started delivering these plagues until Pharaoh finally gave in and let the Jews get the hell out of dodge

Here they are:

1. **Turning water into blood** (rivers of the stuff—yuck!)
2. **Frogs in the house, the bedchamber, the beds, the oven, and even the kneading troughs** (then again, the French may not have minded that last one)
3. **Lice** (and the exact injunction was to turn dust into it, so get out those dust rags again, for more than just your skin cells this time!)
4. **Swarms of flies**
5. **Diseased livestock**
6. **Boils everywhere!**
7. **Hail** (this one, while inconvenient, seems pretty low on the ick factor)
8. **Swarms of locusts** (good for getting rid of tourists, see *Hoarding Together*, pg. 142)
9. **Darkness** (see #7)
10. **Death of the firstborn** (oh, whoops, okay. This just got into the not-funny-but-okay-to-joke-about-because-a-couple-thousand-years-have-gone-by category.)

Hey Gobble, Gobble

President James K. Polk had a dirty job to do—and not just running the country (*wah, wah, wah*). Before he got to the White House, you could find him in the chicken coop assisting with the artificial insemination of turkeys.

Do You Promise to Take a Shower Soon? I Do.

Here comes the bride, carrying a lovely bouquet. What a nice tradition. Umm, not so fast. It actually comes from some nasty bit of history. In the old days, people only took a bath a couple of times a year, and maybe not even for their own wedding. Brides started carrying bouquets down the aisle to cover up their own...

Did You Know? *A bouquet usually refers to a pretty collection of flowers, but it also means an odor.*

Only the Nose Knows

If you think Attila the Hun's massacres make for gruesome reading, did you ever hear how *he* died? Some say he drowned in his own nosebleed. In 2011, a British man died the same way. Doctors think that an intense nosebleed may have led to suffocation.

Left for Dead

Ever heard the expression "dead ringer" to mean someone who really looks a lot like someone else? Well, that sounds harmless enough, but many say the origin of the expression comes from a fear of being buried alive, which led to the practice of putting a bell inside a coffin. If you woke and realized that you'd been left for dead, you would ring the bell. Some say the expression "saved by the bell" originates here, too. Scholars don't agree on those stories, but the fear that motivates them is not unfounded. Before modern medicine, being buried alive wasn't all that uncommon, since people didn't have the equipment we have today to determine when someone's really kicked the bucket. (Although not having a pulse is a pretty good sign—or rather, a pretty bad one.)

Did You Know? *President George Washington (see next page) and the composer Frédéric Chopin (see* **Jar of Hearts,** *pg. 223) both had a particular fear of being buried alive.*

Declaration of Death

We knew the guy had patience ever since his stint at Valley Forge, so maybe it's not surprising that George Washington, our country's first president, waited 12 days after he died to be buried (to make sure he wouldn't be buried alive). The American hero was willing to look death in the face; he just wanted to make sure he didn't have to do it while still alive. (Then again, he's got nothing on a tribe native to Malaysia. See *You've Got All the Time in the World*, pg. 124.)

Oh, My Aching Head. If Only I Could Take a Chunk out.

No compendium of uncivilized history would be complete without a nod to trephination—the practice of drilling a hole into the head in order to remove part of the skull bone. Why would a doctor perform this procedure? Well, if you didn't feel well—like, for example, you had a headache— early surgeons thought this might offer relief. Plus, apparently you got to make a necklace with the severed bone, so that was cool! Show-and-tell to end all show-and-tells. "I've got a headache this big. Oh, I mean, wait a minute." (Move hands a little closer together.) "This big."

AROUND THE
(ROACH-INFESTED)
HOUSE

You don't need to venture far from your bed to find all kinds of stuff fit for your nightmares: cockroaches ready to crawl in your ear as soon as you fall sleep, pests mistaken for pets (millipede, tarantulas, and lizards—all popular in various countries), hidden animal parts in everything from plastic bags to toothpaste, and candles that smell like hamburgers. Oh, and let's not forget the dust on the coffee table—most of it flaked off your skin. Come along for a tour through a house of horrors—your own.

Dead Skin Cells

Do you feel like your parents are constantly asking you to dust the furniture, even though you just did? (And shouldn't you get an increase in your allowance sometime soon?) When you're eye level with dust bunnies galore, you may find yourself wondering where all that dust came from, anyway. Well, four fifths of it came from your body. So if your mom says you really should pitch in more, tell her you are, by letting your skin cells land where they may. You're the one who created a lot of that mess in the first place—without even trying.

Sunny Sides up

How about scrambled eggs for breakfast? If you're lucky, you'll get one of the rare mutant eggs floating around that contain multiple yokes. A woman once found five of them in a single eggshell. Guess that egg-white-only diet is going straight out the farmhouse window.

Did You Know? If eggs are fresh, they sink in water. Throw away any eggs that float.

Snap, Crackle, Poof

t's not an old wives' tale. The gassiest foods are the notorious offenders: beans, broccoli, cabbage, onions, and brussels sprouts. Fruit and whole wheat produce their fair share of flatulence, too. Of course, those with lactose intolerance start the horn section after a simple snack of milk or cheese.

Did You Know? We love omelets as much as the next guys and gals, but we have to admit that this is kind of disturbing. The eggs we eat are technically chicken menstruation. The chickens kept for hatching eggs for human consumption don't mingle with roosters; hence, there's no danger of fertilization. Technically, it's the same thing as when a female of our species has her period.

GROSS GIFT IDEAS (THESE ALL REALLY EXIST!)

- Squirrel-foot earrings
- Fetus-shaped cookie cutters
- Toilet-bowl mug
- Pooze—fart noisemaker (a kind of gooey clay that makes a sound like someone breaking wind)
- Underwear built for two (we don't want to try to visualize this)
- A dead-rat thong

And, of course, there's the old standby, the whoopee cushion. Instead of the usual gag of putting it on someone's chair, why not try this variation. Keep the cushion under your shirt at the table at a dinner party. When the room is quiet, jump up and make a dash for the bathroom, bent over and complaining that your stomach hurts. Leave a trail of firecrackers as you go.

What Me Worry? I Scurry.

If you step on a cockroach, listen for the crunch (and sometimes a smell). Then watch it go running off again. They're hearty little critters—after all, their ancestors survived whatever it is that wiped out the dinosaurs (see *Planet of the Roaches*, pg. 131).

Wiping around the World

Besides your everyday T.P. (toilet paper), the following objects have all been used to wipe someone's nether regions at one time or another: seaweed, moss, mussel shells, grass, clay, stone, snow, corncobs, a bidet, a sponge on the end of a stick, wool. Many cultures still use the bare hand.

50 = the number of pounds of toilet paper an average American flushes away every year.

 **IN THE KNOW**

A letter in your mailbox:
a polite way of saying you
have a wedgie (which is a
semipolite way of saying your
pants are tucked into your
butt)

Home Sweet Onion

When there's no White Castle in walking distance and you just can't get your hands on what you crave, maybe the smell alone will satisfy. In the spring of 2010, White Castle created a burger-scented candle in honor of National Cheeseburger Month. Proceeds went to...autism research? Hmmm, okay. Apparently the 10,000 red meat and onion smell delight sold so fast, they ran out.

Straight from the Cow's Behind

Ah—that nice, woody smell of a fresh layer of mulch around the pine trees in the front yard. Just what is in that nutrient-rich material? All kinds of stuff—it could include leaves, bark, timber, and even manure. So your yard is covered with cow poop? It just might be.

Headless Roachman

Where's my head? A cockroach may wonder that—for up to a month before he finally bites the dust. Then again, a headless cockroach sounds better to us than the intact variety. At least they can't bite.

Grand Entrance

You emerge from the bathroom, your face positively radiant with your new rosy blush and shimmery lip gloss, only to have your pesky brother ask, "Hey, did you just fard?" What an idiot! Wait—maybe you misheard him. He said, "fard" not "fart." Props to him for memorizing this week's vocab list. Fard means to coat your face with makeup, from the German "*faro*," meaning colored.

Did You Know? Most people use their left hand to wipe their bottom. (Aren't you glad you shake hands using your right?)

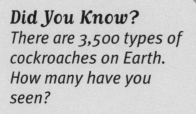

Did You Know?
There are 3,500 types of cockroaches on Earth. How many have you seen?

Got Roach?

Scientists believe that cockroaches might bite you in your sleep if you lie still enough (maybe restless leg syndrome isn't so bad after all). But it gets worse. If you have a sudden pain in your ear, it may not be your standard ear infection. Cockroaches have been known to climb into people's ears while they're asleep. Forceps are used to remove them. (Don't try it at home.)

Ring around the Ringworm

Ringworms can really get under your skin, but some people swear by a fairly easy way to kill them—which is pretty gross, in our opinion. They trace around the infected area with a pen enough times that they block it from moving so that it eventually dies. But then how do you dig it out? Maybe the best thing to do is to see a doctor.

Be an Expert! *Ringworm is caused by a fungus.*

Old MacDonald Hid a Farm

You may have heard that animal bones are used in JELL-O™ and cornbread mixes, but did you know that animal parts are commonly used in plastic bags, fireworks, tires, fabric softener, shampoo, and toothpaste as well? (For more on secret ingredients, see *Roses Are Red, and so Are Some Bugs*, pg. 141.)

What the Fungi!

It sounds gross, but what are fungi exactly? They're parasitic plant organisms that can grow without sunlight. Mold, yeast, and mildew are all various types of fungi. Some attach themselves to your bathtub and some to your body! The cell walls of fungi differ from cell walls in plants in that they contain chitin rather than cellulose. Not all fungi are bad, however. What about mushrooms on your pizza? They're a kind of fungus! Stay away from the poisonous death cap variety, however, as they're easily confused with the Paddy Straw.

All Set for Baby

When setting up a nursery for a baby, one would be ill advised to copy a fly. They tend to lay their eggs in rather unpleasant places like manure or meat. Sometimes botfly eggs even hatch in a human being's skin, popping out when they're fully formed maggots.

Did You Know? *You may be scared of your neighbor's Rottweiler, but if you live in NYC, you're more likely to be bitten by a rat than a dog. About 300 people are bitten annually in the city. Where's that Rat Whisperer when you need him?*

Cheese, Please—and Don't Forget the Bacteria

Many people know that blue cheese or gorgonzola contains mold—but there's bacteria in every kind of cheese; that's how it's made, by adding bacteria to milk. In Swiss cheese, the carbon dioxide gas created by the bacteria *Propionibacterium shermanni* creates the signature holes.

Be an Expert! Food poisoning is most often caused by salmonella bacteria.

What Part about Dessert Did You not Understand?

There's always room for JELL-O, but not if it's mixed with lettuce and cucumbers! In the 1950s, JELL-O salad was commonplace—and not the yummy marshmallow and cherry kind you may have tried at your great aunt Bessie's summer picnic. Gracing the tables of Leave it to Beaver-type dining-room tables was a real salad—carrots, celery, radishes—mixed in with lemon JELL-O. And even that's not as weird as some of the actual flavors they once had: Italian salad, coffee, celery, and tomato were all once bona fide flavors. What a surprise they didn't catch on!

Passing on Bacteria

Disposable diapers are an environmental hazard, but they save parents from the hazardous fact that washing machines don't always kill the bacteria on soiled underwear. Of course, that's no help for those of us who use the public laundromat (and the gross part isn't what's in your bag on laundry day, but what was in the machine before you used it). On the flip side, the number of disposable diapers piling up in landfills is pretty terrifying, too (see *Earth, Breaking Wind, and Fire*, pg. 68).

World's Grossest Pets

Come on, people—did you miss the part about how pets are meant to be fluffy and cute? You're supposed to want to cuddle with them and *pet* them; that's how they got the name! Here are some pets people insist on keeping:

• Tarantula (don't let it escape!)
• Madagascar hissing cockroach (this hisser can grow up to 4 inches long)
• Millipede
• Walking stick or stick insect
• Snake
• Giant rat (see **Monster Rat**, pg. 56)
• Rabbits (disclaimer: they're adorable, but some people object to the endless streams of excrement)

(For more on roaches as pets, see **Here, Little Roachie**, pg. 93. Or you can opt to eat them instead. For candy ones, see **Halloween High Jinks,** pg.78. But maybe you're up for the real thing. If so, check out **Mouthwatering Frights**, pg. 18.)

If your parents won't let you have a pet, at least you've always got your eyelash mites. For more on these tiny critters, see **I See You**, pg. 202.

ECO-
UNFRIENDLY

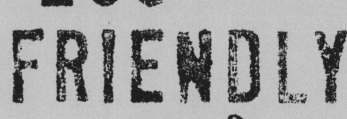

As gross as the stuff in your house may be, what's out there—in the neighborhood pool, the ocean, and even outer space—will give you a real case of the heebie-jeebies—or, as the British say, the screaming habdabs.

Better Luck in Your Next Life

People routinely die on their way up Mount Everest and are often left there, frozen for eternity—sometimes right near the trail where others continue to make their way. As of 2010, there were over 100 bodies scattered around in what's known as the "death zone," many quite well-preserved.

Amount of Pee in Public Pools

You may not love the taste of chlorine, but be glad it's there to keep things tidy. Approximately one-fifth of the swimmers in public pools admit to peeing while swimming.

Chemical Warfare

Thank goodness for chlorine in public pools, which combats the ick factor of doing the doggy paddle in water mixed with urine (see last page) and a host of other bodily fluids. Still, it's a bit disturbing to find out that chlorine is a poisonous gas that was used by the Germans in WWI. Being gassed by chlorine is a painful way to go. French victims died slowly as the chemical destroyed their lungs, until a lack of oxygen finally did them in.

Sticky Sidewalks

Have you ever heard someone tell you that chewing gum lasts forever in your belly? That's not true. Though swallowing excessive amounts could lead to problems, a piece or two—while not recommended—will get broken down eventually. A glop that flops onto the sidewalk, by contrast, is there for good, or at least until someone scrapes it off, a process that costs the government a fair amount of money. Petrochemicals make chewing gum sticky enough to adhere to the street. We've all seen the ugly black splotches a piece of Doublemint turns into; they're anything but minty fresh.

Earth-Friendly Flush

Here's a brief (coarse) course in an ecological approach to flushing your toilet: If it's yellow, let it mellow; if it's brown, flush it down.

Space Junk

It may be out of sight, out of mind for some of us, but the litter in space is starting to worry scientists. Right now, billions of pieces of trash are in orbit around us. And it just keeps getting worse. As Evan I. Schwartz wrote in *Wired* magazine in 2010, "The number of manufactured objects cluttering the sky is now expected to double every few years, as large objects weaken and split apart and new collisions create more...debris, leading to yet more collisions." Unlike the pigpen that somehow passes for your bedroom, this is a mess we really have to clean up!

Be an Expert! *Space debris makes its orbit around Earth at 17,500 miles per hour. That's some fast trash!*

Plastic Land Mass

Out in the middle of the North Pacific Ocean is a pile of garbage so massive, it's estimated to be at least as big as the state of Texas, if not double the size. The Great Eastern Garbage Patch is a collection of debris reined in by a gyre. As far back as 1988, the National Oceanic and Atmospheric Administration wrote a paper forecasting its existence.

IN THE KNOW

Gyre: an ocean current shaped in a vortex pattern

Bring the Jungle in

Sure, bugs and pillow mites are unpleasant, but for the most part, harmless. Rather than worry about a daddy longlegs staring at you from the window ledge, worry about actual poison around your house in synthetic materials, harsh chemicals, and mold. You can easily improve indoor air quality the natural way. Crysanthemums, the lovely fall flower, are great air purifiers. English ivy and lady palm, as well as peace lilies, will all help cut down on toxins in your house. Bamboo plants target formaldehyde.

BARBARIC
BODIES

A 19th-century nursery rhyme describes girls as being made of sugar and spice and everything nice and boys of frogs and snails and puppy-dogs' tails. Neither is quite on the mark, but the description for boys comes closer to the truth. You don't have to go far—in fact, you don't have to go anywhere—to find some of the yuckiest stuff around; the human body produces all kinds of slimy, germy-ridden stuff. Plus, it's absolutely crawling with bacteria. Take any body part—even an eyelash—put it under a microscope, and you'll swear you're watching *Gremlins*.

Shall I Compare Thee to a Summer's Day?

Here are just a few of the gross things found in or on the human body: zits, boils, carbuncles, bile, pus, scabs, sweat, blood, snot, mucus, and eye gunk. Oh, and moles. Is a hairy mole still considered a beauty mark? (Maybe it depends on how the hair is styled.)

Watery Feces by Any Other Name Would Smell as Terrible

You know how Alaskans (supposedly) have dozens of words for snow? Well, there's a tribe in South America that has dozens of words for...diarrhea. There are a few colorful expressions for it in English as well. The squirts, colon blow, Delhi belly, Aztec two step, the runs, anal leak, and the scoots. And, of course, there's that disgusting crossover use for when someone won't stop talking: "verbal diarrhea."

Did You Know? *What's the sweatiest part of your body? Your feet? Armpits? Groin area? Back? Forehead? Nope, it's usually your hands!*

Be an Expert! *What is diarrhea? It's your body's attempt to clean out something that has bacteria or was too spicy for your body to tolerate. In most cases, water is removed from food in the large intestines, but in the case of the food, your body wants it out of there fast, so more water joins the log flume, and out it goes.*

There's a Hair in My Mouth
—and It's Supposed to Be There!

Your tongue is covered with microvilli—tiny projections from the cells that make up your taste buds. Those little hairs are the vehicle for transporting info to your brain about what you are tasting.

Furry Lingua

There is a condition where your tongue grows lots of black, icky hair that is NOT supposed to be there. It's called *lingua villosa nigra*—literally, black, hairy tongue. Smoking, not cleaning your mouth well enough, and certain mouth rinses are all associated risk factors. According to the Mayo Clinic, "an overgrowth of bacteria" leads to a tongue with "a dark, furry appearance." The good news is it's easy to treat. Maybe you don't even have to tell anyone you have it. If you feel like leaking word of your unusual condition, bite your tongue!

"Man is a museum of diseases,
a home of impurities; he comes today
and is gone tomorrow; he begins as dirt
and departs as stench."
—MARK TWAIN

Drink Water, Smell Better

Dehydration is one of the leading causes of bad breath (hence, the champion dragon of morning breath, coming after 6–8 hours of decreased saliva production). Low-carb diets can contribute to monster breath as well, due to ketones released when your body "breaks down fat." What about chronic bad breath? That's called halitosis.

Wash that Hair Right offa Your Head

If your shower drain seems to be clogged with hair after every shampoo, don't stress (which might only cause more hair loss). On average, humans lose between 50 – 100 hairs a day. So don't pull your hair out, but do clean the drain!

Did You Know? The longest ear hairs ever recorded were 6 inches each. Sew them together and you could make some nice socks!

Creative Ways to Say "Fart"

Break Wind   Pass Gas   Toot

One-Man Salute   Anal Volcano

Airbrush Your Boxers   Flatulate

Jam Tart   Blast the Butt Trumpet

Cut the Cheese   Quacking Ducks

Drop a Bomb   Let it Rip

Beef

Hold Your Tongue

The old wives' tale that people have died by swallowing their tongues is not true. The frenulum underneath the tongue holds it firmly—if flexibly—in place.

The Virtues of Earwax

Doctors recommend letting earwax, like an annoying houseguest, leave on its own time rather than clearing it out with a cotton swab. Unlike the second-cousin twice removed, the wax is there for a reason, namely to keep bacteria and dirt out of your ear. It protects against creepy crawlies creeping in there, too, but not in every case (see *Got Roach?* pg. 178). So let the wax and the guest stay, although you may remind the latter of Benjamin Franklin's clever line: "Fish and visitors smell in three days." Then again, the guest may simply respond by saying fish sounds like a great idea for dinner.

Did You Know? *Burping is a rather inefficient process—you swallow air every time you belch.*

GROSS BODY STATISTICS

21,575	= average number of farts issued from a single butt in a lifetime
⅓ pound	= daily poop output
60,000 miles	= how long your blood vessels would be if you laid them end to end
1 quart	= amount of snot swallowed daily
7.5 grams	= combined weight of your eyebrows
10 pounds	= weight of your skin

Flatulence Habit

On average, humans fart about 14 times a day, with no significant difference in output between genders. There are certain products on the market meant to reduce emissions, and others that block the fumes of the ones that do slip out.

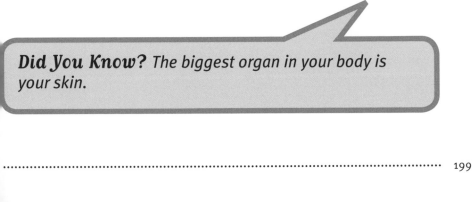

Did You Know? *The biggest organ in your body is your skin.*

Piggy-Tails

The hairs inside your nose are there for a reason. They're there to stop germs and dirt from getting in. That doesn't mean when they're long enough to braid that you're immune from all diseases, so keep those clippers handy.

All Along the Pipeline

It depends where you are along the pipeline, but you're dealing with the same thing whether you're a proctologist (if you don't know what that is, here's a hint: *proktos* means "anus" in Greek) or a plumber. Then again, even a gourmet chef has a place on the gastrointestinal track. After all, what goes out must come in.

Be an Expert! *Have you ever noticed that your pee is unusually dark yellow? It could be a sign that you are dehydrated. If it doesn' t have enough water, your body revisits the urine it was going to release and gathers every last drop it can. What remains has a higher concentration than usual of the stuff your body doesn' t want.*

Fab Scabs

Scabs are especially yucky when separated from the body —which is always a risk when you pick at them—but they're an essential and fascinating part of the body's healing process. How do they form? When you get a cut, blood leaks out (or rushes out, depending on the size of the scrape). Platelets in the blood collect at the exit to block the bleeding, and threads of something called fibrin create a net. Red and white blood cells get caught in the net and pile up until a clot (a soft lump) forms. Eventually, the clot hardens into a scab, which feels like a very tough piece of skin. The scab is sort of like an umbrella, keeping the open area clean and dry while new skin grows.

I See You

Eyelash mites eat the oil and dead skin around and in your eyes. They don't seem to bother most people, but experts disagree as to their role in diseases. Some people may have allergies or weakened immune systems, which leave them vulnerable to various disorders caused by these critters which are known to inch across your face while you sleep.

Do Your Ears Swing Low?

Is it true that ears never stop growing? Preliminary research suggests that they keep growing until you die. Many claim your nose and feet do as well. If your feet grow at the same rate as you shrink with age, your total length will stay the same.

Boogie-Loogie

The word "loogie" isn't used as much as it once was. We've really only ever heard it used in the expression "hock a loogie," which means to spit a great big glob of mucus. The expression itself is a nice little lesson in etymology. "Hock" is onomatopoeic, meaning that it's meant to sound like what it refers to. "Loogie," a combination of the two words "lung" and "cookie" (in both meaning and sound), is a portmanteau. Who said you couldn't impress your English teacher while secretly memorizing gross facts?

A Frog in Your Throat

Got phlegm in your throat? You may have post-nasal drip! What happens is that the nasal tissues are overproducing mucus that then creeps its way down toward your tonsils. And it can lead to some pretty serious dragon breath!

IN THE KNOW

Blow chunks: to hurl, throw up, lose your lunch, spew. Any way you say it, it's how you do it that matters. The expression is so horrific, it could be the basis of a new figure of speech, like an onomatopoeia, but instead of sounding like what it is, hearing the word makes you do the thing it describes.

Lucky Upchuck

Throwing up is pretty gross, but it is how your body gets rid of something that's not good for it. Better out than in.

Hot-Shot Snot

Do you envy the cheetah for its speed? For short distances, those wild cats can reach about 80 miles per hour. But even if your legs can't carry you even one-tenth as fast, your snot may be in the running. A good *ah-choo* can send those mucus particles flying at an average speed of 60 miles per hour. That's nothing to sneeze at.

Bloody Tears

or real-life viruses that sound like horror movies, nothing beats Ebola hemorrhagic fever caused by the Ebola virus, which causes the victim to bleed uncontrollably, even through the eyes. (There's an animal that does this naturally, o scare away predators. See *Did You Know* about the horny oad, pg. 46.)

What is Belly Lint Made of?

Well, as the name suggests, there's lint in there. Dirt creeps n as well, combining with sweat, dead skin cells, and your clothing lint to create that peculiar kind of stored debris. Of ourse, most of us don't store it for long. It comes out easily

Did You Know? *Hemophilia is a blood disorder in which the blood doesn't clot. If a hemophiliac gets cut, the blood just keeps pouring out. The word is a little odd in our opinion. It comes from the Greek* hemo, *meaning "blood," and phlein, "to love."*

in the bath or shower and you can use a little powder to keep in dry during the day. Then again, there are the rare individuals who choose to save belly-button lint (see *Gross Collections*, pg. 98).

"Your skin is the only thing keeping all of the oozing, pulsating guts and goop inside you from slopping into a big wet pile on the ground."
—BART KING

House of Horrors

Every square inch of human skin is host to 100,000 bacteria. But before you go running to the doctor, keep in mind that most of these are helpful. Either way, though, our skin is literally *crawling* with parasites.

Did You Know? *The Ebola virus is named for the river in Africa in the Democratic Republic of the Congo.*

Sour Feet

People always say to make lemonade out of lemons, but what happens after you drink it? Not all the lemonade you guzzle back comes out as pee. Have you ever removed your socks on a hot day to find that they are soaking wet? It turns out your feet can produce a pint of sweat a day. That's the equivalent of two cups of liquid just from those tired dogs; so on the dog days of summer, make sure you drink up so you don't get dehydrated. (See *Drink Water, Smell Better*, pg. 196.)

IN THE KNOW

Dogs: (slang) feet, primarily used in the expression "My dogs are tired."

Did You Know? Need a haircut? Be glad it grows mostly on your head. Until about 100,000 years ago, humans walked around with thick hair all over their bodies (not unlike some other mammals you may have seen).

One and Only You (and Your B.O.)

If you sometimes feel like you're not very unique, remember that everyone has their own distinct and one-of-a-kind smell. Your dog knows what it is. Let's make sure your your friends don't.

Waste Factory

Yes, it's true, not only does everyone—from peasant to princess—go number two, pretty much everyone has number two inside their body most of the time.

Smelly Belly

If farts and poop smell so bad, and they come out of your body, does that mean the inside of your body...Yep, you guessed it—it smells terrible.

Excuse Me for that Eructation

When in polite company, maybe it's best to refer to burping by its clinical name of "eructation." People will be so thrown off by the word choice that they'll forget the act that preceded it. (Then again, it may be that, like Shakespeare's rose, "A burp by any other name will smell as bad." Plus eructation can also refer to the actual substance that shoots back up your throat when you burp. Hmmm, on second thought, maybe you're better off just burping and not drawing any more attention to the act.)

You might want to remember this poetic apology if you burp in polite company:

> "Excuse me, excuse me
> from the bottom of my heart.
> If it came out the other way,
> it would have been a fart."

Lighten up

Do people ever tell you to lighten up? Tell them you will—when you die. The average cremated body weighs a mere 10 pounds or less.

Be an Expert! *An Arab physician named Abulcasis, who died in 1013, was the first person in the medical field to document the symptoms of hemophilia.*

THE GROSSOPHILE'S GUIDE TO BEING GREEN AND THRIFTY

When it comes to consumption these days, organic, green, and cheap are all the rage. So the next time you've bankrupted your piggy bank, try these eco-friendly solutions—they're not only homemade, —they're *human*-made.

- Earwax candles
- Belly-lint baby blanket
- Tear salt (get kosher from your local synagogue)
- Hair rugs

People drink urine in a pinch, but that's a little far out for our taste. If your feet are pressing out 2 cups of liquid a day (See *Sour Feet*, pg. 207), why waste it?

Deep-Sea Gas

You hear a lot about how great omega-3s are for you, and one way to get them is through fish oil supplement. But unfortunately, that's not the omega (end) of it. The burps are rather fish-infused, especially from cheaper brands. To minimize the effect, take them with food and make sure your brand is "pharmaceutical grade."

Shower Power

Why do shower farts smell worse than farts in other places? Some attribute the power of the shower fart to the confined space, and some to the humidity, which traps smells (just like on a hot day in a city). Most experts agree that they don't necessarily smell any differently, but more of the smell from the gas factory hits your olfactory senses.

I Know What You Had for Dinner Last Summer

Is it true that garlic gets sweated out through your pores and that others can smell it? Yes. So if people seem to be giving you a wide birth after your pesto dinner, you'll know why. Asparagus, of course, is notorious for making your pee smell like...well, asparagus.

Erin Go All out

St. Patrick's Day means cornbeef and cabbage...and, if you're really feeling festive, something with green food coloring which will even alter the color of what lands in the toilet.

TRUE OR FALSE?

You should pop a blister?
False. It's better to let it deflate and heal on its own rather than risk infection.

Heavy earrings can stretch out your earlobes?
True.

Poop sometimes floats?
True. Ironically, this is often the result of eating an excess of fatty foods.

Secondhand clothing can bring bugs into the home?
True. As soon as you buy some, store the clothes in a plastic bag tied shut for a week or two.

I'll Have What He's Having

Do grown-ups ever drink human milk? Yes, apparently it's quite common for new fathers to sample their newborn's dinner.

FARTS & CULTURE

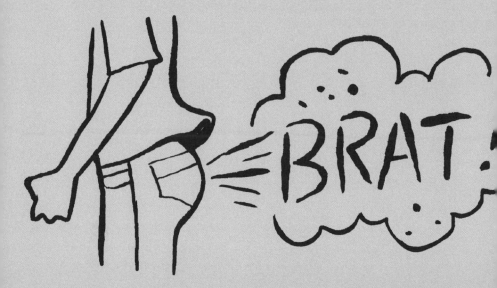

From high art (the witches' stew in *Macbeth*) to low (a fart joke or two), and everything in between, explore these uncouth and foul displays of creativity. Maybe Lady Gaga's meat dress or the dead body exhibit will inspire you to make your own repulsive artwork.

Big Slug Love

If you're a slug fan, Susan Pearson has some advice for you in *How to Teach a Slug to Read*. For starters, find books he'll like, such as *Rhymes from Mother Slug*, *A Tale of Two Termites* or *Hug a Bug*. Have you ever thought about what a snail would look like without its shell? You guessed it... probably an awful lot like a slug.

Cow Power

Pop singer Lady Gaga once wore a dress of raw meat to the Video Music Awards. She had previously worn a similar grubby garb for *Vogue Hommes Japan*. She won an award for her video of "Bad Romance"—we're guessing any date you show up to wearing raw meat is not likely to end very well. (What happened to the dress? Don't worry, even if you missed Gaga that night, you can still catch the piece of meat on display at the Rock n' Roll Hall of Fame in Cleveland, Ohio.)

Gross Band Names
(These are all real bands!)

Fartbarf   Regurgitator

The Pooh Sticks   Pissing Razors

Cannibal Corpse   Lungbutter

Victoria's Secretions

Pukesnake   Lost Underpants of Doom

And, perhaps our
all-time favorite—
Screaming Headless Torsos

Nipple Craze

Bizarre fashion took a giant leap forward when designer Rachel Freire showcased an outfit made of 3,000 nipples taken from cows and yaks. Reactions were mixed, even among advocates for the right to breastfeed in public.

 IN THE KNOW

Yak: a shaggy bovine found in Asia

I've Got My Eye on You

In Pritzker Park in Chicago, Illinois, there's a three-story-high sculpture of a giant eyeball, blood vessels and all. It's supposedly modeled after the artist's own peepers. If you're in the Windy City, make sure you get an eyeful.

Did You Know? *There are people whose job it is to make fake eyeballs for people to wear. They're called ocularists. Whoever said an art degree wasn't useful? (For other job ideas, see* **Careers for Grossophiles,** *pg. 101.)*

Stone-Cold Killer

Talk about a bad hair day. The mythical beast Medusa had serpents for hair, but that's not all. One look at her could turn you into stone. Luckily for the rest of us, she was beheaded by Perseus.

A River Has the Runs

In Dante's *Divine Comedy*, there's nothing funny about the poop bobbing around the River Styx. That could lead to some serious hepatitis! Then again, the people down there were already in hell, so maybe it didn't matter all that much.

Eternal Bark

Take plenty of pictures of Fluffy while he's alive; but if you tend to misplace your camera, you can always turn to the Scandinavian design company Skrekkøgle after your pet has died. They'll take the ashes from a cremated kitty or pooch and transform them into a photograph. Horror movies merge with reality: That piece of artwork hanging in the dining room doesn't just look like your best friend, it *is* him.

BOOKS FOR GROSSOPHILES

Why Do Flies Eat Doggy Poop? And Other Poems by L.W. Lewis
Mystery Meat: Hot Dogs, Sausages, and Lunch Meats: The Incredibly Disgusting Story by Stephanie Watson
Yuck! A Big Book of Little Horrors by Robert Snedden
Fear Factor: Yuck! Grossest Stunts Ever! by Jesse Leon McCann and Randi Reisfeld
Yuck! Icky, Sticky, Gross Stuff in Your Garden by Pam Rosenberg and Beatrix Helena Ramos
Grossology and You by Sylvia Branzei and Jack Keely
Kama Pootra: 52 Mind-Blowing Ways to Poop by Daniel Cole Young
The Fart Without Fear Cookbook by Wayne Chen and Gary Goss

Experimental Art

The Holy Virgin Mary painting was a controversial piece of art by British artist Chris Ofili that used real elephant droppings layered over a painting of a black Virgin Mary. The curious collage came through New York in 1999 as part of an exhibition called "Sensation," which caused quite a stir—even leading to a lawsuit. Mayor Rudy Giuliani in particular thought he smelled something rotten near Prospect Park.

I'd Know that Smell Anywhere...

James Joyce is recognized as one of the most brilliant writers of the 20th century. But that didn't get in the way of his self-proclaimed ability to recognize the smell of his girlfriend's farts anywhere. Okay, that is just *way* too much information for our taste, which is how many people felt when James Joyce's private letters were published in 1975. Even the worst episode of *Fear Factor* can't rival real life. In Joyce's most famous work *Ulysses*, the main character enjoys a hint of urine in his breakfast food. This guy had some seriously twisted ideas.

Natural Wax

Have you ever visited a wax museum? There are plenty of them around, featuring lifelike sculptures of celebrities made entirely of wax. Many have thought of it, but so far no one has created a sculpture made entirely of earwax. Maybe you can be the first!

Be an Expert! *In the 1953 horror movie* House of Wax, *things really got creepy. The professor's realistic wax sculptures turned out to be the bodies of people he killed and covered in wax. No wonder they looked so realistic! (Not to mention, the film was one of the first to be produced in 3-D. Look out!)*

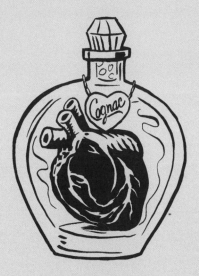

Jar of Hearts

The great Polish composer Frédéric Chopin was creative in death as well as in life. In his will, he requested to be cut open before burial to be sure he was actually dead. His last words were said to be, "The earth is suffocating....Swear to make them cut me open, so that I won't be buried alive." In the end, his heart wasn't buried at all, but removed from his body and preserved in a jar filled with cognac. (No connection to the Christina Perri pop song "Jar of Hearts.")

TONGUE TIED
Try saying this fast, three times in a row:

"One smart fellow, he felt smart.
Two smart fellows, they both felt smart.
Three smart fellows, they all felt smart."

Okay—now how smart to you feel?

Fresh Delivery

It may sound cute to take a nap with Nemo (other than the fact that you and Nemo can't breathe in the same element), but "sleeping with the fishes" means something rather sinister—lying at the bottom of the ocean. In the book and movie *The Godfather*, Luca Brasi's killers send the Corleones his body armor wrapped around a fish, a clear Sicilian message that signifies he's "sleeping with the fishes," or simply put, dead.

Under Your Skin

We're all the same underneath our skin, right? Well, now you can actually conduct some research on the matter. Check out BODIES. The Exhibition in New York, Atlanta, or Las Vegas, where real bodies are preserved by a process of plastination and put on display for your viewing pleasure. Many visitors report being scared straight by seeing how organs decay when exposed to smoke or excessive alcohol. Though some consider it a CSI-inspired freak show, the exhibit is meant to be educational and the website recommends it for kids. (There has, however, been a certain amount of controversy over the matter that the bodies were not donated, and their owners may not have intended to be hung up on view for eternity.)

Sweet Nightmares

You want to hear gross stories? You don't have to look much further than your average nursery rhyme or fairy tale. "Ring around the Rosy" is about the black plague. The ring was the telltale sign of having contracted the fatal disease. The "pocket full of posies" was supposed to keep you safe. Then comes the climax: "We all fall down." You can easily guess what that refers to (the disease was fatal, meaning that it killed you). And that's all for the one little rhyme! Then there are the blind mice whose tails are chopped off by the farmer's wife with her carving knife. The witch who plans to stick Hansel and Gretel's heads in the oven. And who can forget the wolf that eats Little Red Riding Hood's grandmother? The Brothers Grimm even have a story called "The Girl without Hands." We're pretty sure she gets them back in the end, but that's some rough sledding there for a while.

IN THE KNOW

Rough sledding: expression meaning very challenging situation

The Three Little Assassins

Japanese photographer Miwa Yanagi brings the horror and gruesomeness of fairy tales to life with her disturbing interpretations of children's stories. As artist John Coulthart puts it, Yanagi puts the "grim in the Brothers Grimm." (But take a second look at any of the stories—or see *Sweet Nightmares* above—and you'll see that the tales are pretty disturbing all on their own.)

HEAD CHOPPER

"The Bells of St. Clements" is a pleasant little English children's song. If you still have your mouth intact (see below), sing along! Just duck when you get to the last line.

Oranges and lemons say the bells of
  St. Clement's,
You owe me five farthings say the bells
  of St. Martin's,
When will you pay me? say the bells of
  Old Bailey,
When I grow rich say the bells of
  Shoreditch,
When will that be? say the bells of
  Stepney,
I do not know say the great bells of
  Bow,
Here comes a candle to light you to bed,
And here comes a chopper to chop off
  your head!"

Heading My Way?

We've probably all heard of John the Baptist, but his severed head may be even more famous than the rest of him. In the New Testament, it was served up on a platter to Herod's daughter, Salome. The butchering was her mother's idea, clear evidence that mother doesn't always know best. Excavators think that they may have recently come upon the famous skull under a fourth-century Byzantine church.

POTTY HUMOR

Here's one you can tell your friends (and hopefully no one will have the bad sense to re-enact it.)

Tommy: "Did you poop in your pants?"

Jim: "No."

Tommy: "Yes, you did."

Jim: "Did not."

Jim and Tommy begin to wrestle until a piece of poop rolls out of Jim's pant leg.

Tommy: "Told you!"

Jim: "Oh! I thought you meant today."

Eerie Gift

Van Gogh is renowned for his artistic vision, but his severed ear receives almost as much attention as his *Starry Night* painting. There is even a café in the U.S. named after it—Van Gogh's Ear Café in Union, New Jersey! Like many geniuses of history, Van Gogh was part crazy-talented and part just-plain-crazy. The self-mutilation story goes that Vincent used a razor to slide of his left earlobe and handed it to a local woman. More recently, scholars have pointed to evidence that another creative visionary, Paul Gauguin, is at least partly responsible for lopping off Gogh's famous lobe.

Gross Word Contest

Someone once started a blog called The World's Grossest Words. They asked readers to rate the grossness of words like "soft turd," "beefy pimple," "barf spray," and "bug squirt." The writer only posted one entry before apparently abandoning the entire idea. Maybe they got too grossed out! Taking up where he or she left off, we've come up with a list of words we find inherently yucky: phlegm, moist, smear, secrete, gyrate, yeast, viscous, squishy, mucus, scummy.

Eye See You One Grisly Murder and Raise You One Blinding

CSI, Law and Order, and *Forensic Files* don't have the patent on gory entertainment. In Sophocles' famous play "Oedipus Rex (Oedipus the King)", written and performed over 2,400 years before the first blood-spatter pattern was analyzed on *Primetime,* our hero kills his father and marries his mother. But that's not the part that will send you running for the upchuck bucket. In the end, Oedipus stabs himself in the eyes with a pin from his dead (oh yeah, forgot to say, she kills herself) mother's dress.

A Little to the Left

If your parents were indie rockers, you may know The Pixies song "Debaser" from the album *Doolittle.* One of the world's all-time grossest lyrics: "Slicing up eyeballs, I want you to know" refer to the 1929 movie by Luis Buñuel and Salvador Dalí called *Un Chien Andalou,* where in a surreal sequence a woman's eyeballs are sliced open.

Over My Dead Body (or Next to it)

William Faulkner famously said, "The past is never dead. It's not even past." Apparently, his characters felt the same way. As we find out at the end of his Southern Gothic short story "A Rose for Emily," the main character slept for years next to the decaying corpse of a suitor she had killed before he'd had a chance to leave her. Forget the ghost in the closet or monster under the bed—how about the dead body lying beside you! We guess Emily wasn't as easily spooked as some of us.

Be an Expert! *Emily Grierson is the name of the main character in William Faulkner's macabre short story "A Rose for Emily."*

IN THE KNOW

Macabre: ghastly, grisly

Double, Double Toil, and Trouble

Perhaps the all-time most famous stew-that-will-make-you-spew is described by the witches in William Shakespeare's play *Macbeth*, in act IV, scene I. Here's a little taste of what they stirred up: "swelter'd venom," "fillet of a fenny snake," "eye of newt and toe of frog, wool of bat and tongue of dog, adder's tork and blind-worm's sting, lizard's leg and howlet's wing." Don't forget the "liver of blaspheming Jew, gall of goat, and slips of yew" and, of course, the "finger of birth-strangled babe." There are poisoned entrails in there, too—but we're not sure whose. Oh, we almost forgot. It wouldn't be the same without the baboon's blood! Stir it all together and let it soak a while. Then serve with crackers or a hearty French bread.

Did You Know? *Some Freudian dream analysts believe dreams where you are handling poop have to do with anxieties around money.*

GROSS REBELLION

ALL THINGS ANTISEPTIC, SWEET, AND DISCREET

Zen and the Art of Elimination

The Japanese are rather modest when it comes to publi elimination. Many group bathrooms have stall doors tha go all the way to the floor and soothing noises playing i the background to muffle embarrassing sounds.

Careless Scientists Unite

For all those kids out there getting reprimanded fo not paying enough attention in class, remind you teacher about the discovery of penicillin. The history changing *penicillium* fungi was discovered by acciden in 1928 when a petri dish was left open. Sir Alexande Fleming noticed that a bacterium called *Staphylococcus aureus* was being eaten away by a mold that had sprung up. He thought it would have implications for medicine as an anti-bacterial agent, but it was not until 12 years later that scientists were able to

Be an Expert! *A moldy piece of bread generally ruins the whole loaf, but moldy fruit can be picked over. Throw out the spoiled part and wash the rest before you eat it.*

roduce antibiotics for people. Pneumonia and tuberculo-
is, along with other serious and often fatal diseases, have
een significantly contained in countries with access
ɔ antibiotics. The danger now is that bacteria are
rowing resistant to antibiotics. But we'll leave that for a
ross-o-pedia sequel.

World's Friendliest Spider

ext time you're tempted to squish or otherwise get rid of a
pider (and they are pretty gross—did you ever hear the
ne about the golden orb spider who ate a snake? It really
appened!), remember Charlotte from the classic E.B. White
tory, *Charlotte's Web*. Once you read about the brave
pider who helped save Wilbur the pig , you can't
elp but have compassion for the weaver-of-the-orb.

*Be an Expert! Charlotte was a barn spider, scientific
name:* Araneus cavaticus.

Sometimes it's Good to Flip Flop

Athlete's foot might sound like something you want, if you dream of slam-dunking in the NBA, but it's actually a fungu that attacks the feet and is hard to get rid of—returnin, even after treatment. Flip-flops in public showers cut dow on the spread of foot fungi, which is always a good thing.

Circle of Life

Outside of Philadelphia, Pennsylvania, farmers reduce an reuse to great effect by collecting leftover food put out i the trash from their neighbors and giving it to their pigs t eat. (The humans, in turn, wait an appropriate amount o time and then eat the pigs.)

Bloodless Dissection

For every 14-year-old who dreads the day she gets hande a scalpel in a biology lab, here's some good news: Moder technology is making real-life dissection a thing of the pas On the Dissection Alternatives website, students can lear how to "keep frogs in nature, not formaldehyde" by workin in virtual labs on specialized software. Blood and guts without the mess!

Turns out You Can Be too Clean

Hand sanitizers have come into vogue with increased awareness about germs. Some worry, however, that their overuse is undermining our bodies' ability to cope with pathogens and even leading to increases in allergies where the body fights off harmless intruders like peanuts or strawberries.

Clean Getaway

Here's a story about a guy who had a real dirt aversion. After robbing a home in Oregon, this peculiar thief took a shower—in the same home! That's where the cops found him. Getting rid of germs may not have been the best getaway plan.

Becoming Spiderman

The most common treatment for phobias is ERP—Exposure and Response Prevention. Basically, if the sight of a spider makes you weak in the knees, and you wanted to try ERP, the process would go like this. First, you'd view the enemy at a safe distance, maybe across the room. Not hyperventilating yet? Good. Next you take a step closer, take tock, and realize that you're till alive. You keep getting loser, slowly desensitizing ourself to the eight-legged avages with venomous angs, until finally you are etting them crawl all over ou like ants on a picnic lanket. Then again, maybe ou'll opt to skip therapy nd just re-imagine an ffending arachnid as a entle descendent of harlotte's, see *World's riendliest Spider*, pg. 237).

Be an Expert! *The fear of spiders is one of the top 20 most common fears. The number-one fear for most people is... speaking in public! So, if you can go tell a room full of people about something terrifying you just learned in this book, you'll prove yourself to be a courageous soul indeed.*

Did You Know? Spiders in the Fruit Cellar *by Barbara Joosse is a book about a girl whose mom helps her confront her fear of the creepy crawlies in the basement.*

POSTSCRIPT: WHAT IS DISGUST?

"It is obvious that 'obscenity' is not a term capable of exact legal definition; in the practice of the Courts, it means 'anything that shocks the magistrate'."

BERTRAND RUSSELL, *SKEPTICAL ESSAYS* (1928)

Why do things disgust us?

Why do we wrinkle our noses at a foul smell and, if it is bad enough, grab our schnoz and hold it tight?

If you answer, "That response is just built into us," you're right. But that leads us to a more interesting question: "*Why* is disgust built into us?"

It sounds funny, but experts consider disgust one of the basic emotions, along with love, joy, surprise, anxiety/fear, sadness/depression, and anger. (There's still some controversy about exactly which emotions shouldn't be included in the "basic" set, but that question goes beyond the scope of this book.)

So now the question is: What is the evolutionary purpose of us having emotions? Why do we get sad, angry, happy, or scared? Primarily, emotions serve to imprint memory as well as to motivate behavior. Emotions themselves can be placed in the broader category of feelings, which would include, say, being cold or hungry. It's easy to see how being cold or hungry will motivate behavior to alleviate discomfort. If you are cold, you'll seek shelter. If you are hungry, you'll find something to eat (and if you can't think of anything, there are some great ideas in **Bizarre Cuisine** on pg. 15).

Let's start, however, with "imprinting memory." This happens when a powerful emotional experience creates a strong memory in your brain, one you may never forget. As a society, we have some shared times in which all our memories are imprinted. If you are at least 15, you probably remember exactly where you were on September 11, 2001, when you heard about the terrorist attacks in New York City, Washington, DC, and Pennsylvania. Similarly, those over 30 remember where they were when they heard about the *Challenger* explosion, and those 55 or more can recount their whereabouts upon hearing of President John F. Kennedy's assassination. These events become what are called collective "flashbulb memories:" they are ones that people in the United States share.

But these flashbulb memories raise another question: Why do we remember *where* we were when we heard the news?

That's not a relevant fact. But the way we are built is to capture everything that's going on during a highly charged moment and to remember all of it. That way, we have everything in memory and can later review which aspects are relevant in order to protect ourselves against future calamity.

While it may not make immediate sense to have this mechanism active for remembering the *Challenger* explosion if we don't plan on joining the space program, think of it this way. Suppose you are in the wilds and a tiger comes charging at you and you survive. Wouldn't it be helpful to collect all the information you can to help you secure advance warning of a future attack? Perhaps certain smells, sounds of small animals scurrying away, proximity to the tree line, and so on might all be clues you could use in the future. What a great mechanism to have your brain capture it all, like a YouTube video, for review, so you can protect yourself in the future. It's the same mechanism at work with the attacks of 9/11, even though, in that case, you won't ultimately need as much data to protect yourself in the future.

Okay, so that's the memory part of emotions. How about the part about organizing and motivating behavior? Let's start by looking at anxiety. It's easy to see that this emotion is designed to alert us to danger. It is also aversive, which generates a strong motivation to get rid of the anxiety and thereby get out of danger. (Sometimes anxiety is a false alarm; there is no real danger, but we are anxious nonetheless, see Introduction, pg. 8.) Disgust serves to alert us to something potentially harmful; something that could make us sick, generally. We often obtain the "disgusting" information via our sense of smell; this accounts for the characteristic expression of disgust, which includes a wrinkled nose. (All basic emotions have characteristic expressions in humans that are recognizable across cultures and time, and which others can readily recognize. So emotions have yet another function as communication devices and regulators of interpersonal relations.)

It's important to have disgust built in to keep us away from things that are dangerous and may make us sick. It's also important to have the memory component so that if a certain food makes you sick and you throw up, the strong memory of being sick should discourage your from returning to that food (Although this is not always the case—see *Lessons from a Rat*, pg. 87).

ometimes things are inherently disgusting and will harm
ll humans. But at other times we develop a disgust
esponse because of what we are taught. So there are
differences in what disgusts people in different cultures.
Some things that Americans find disgusting are commonplace elsewhere (and some of those are included in this
volume). Similarly, some things we take for granted are
considered disgusting in other parts of the world. So,
remember, when we list some practices from other countries
that we find disgusting, even when we do so with a wink,
it's really only our way of looking at things. And all of us,
here and abroad, would be better off if we learned more
about each other's ways, instead of wrinkling our collective
noses at them.

But for now, we hope you have wrinkled, retched, writhed,
and relished the incredible diversity of all things gross,
rude, offensive, vulgar, disgusting, unrefined, and un-
savory contained in this obscene volume.

SELECTED BIBLIOGRAPHY

Buckley, Dr. James, Robert Stremme. *Scholastic Book of Lists: Fun Facts, Weird Trivia, and amazing lists of nearly everything you need to know.* Scholastic Reference, 2006

Deary, Terry. *Horrible History of the World.* Scholastic, 2006

Faulkner, William. *"A Rose for Emily".* Forum, 1930

Ferguson, *Kitty Pythagoras.* Icon Books Ltd, 2011

Hemingway, Ernest. *Death in the Afternoon.* Charles Scribner's Sons, 1932

King, Bart. *The Big Book of Gross Stuff.* Gibbs Smith, 2010

Marlos, Daniel. *The Curious World of Bugs: The Bugman's Guide to the Mysterious and Remarkable Lives of Things That Crawl.* Perigee Trade, 2010

Masoff, Joy. *Oh Yuck! The Encyclopedia of Everything Nasty.* Workman Publishing Company, 2000

McDonald, Megan. *Stink-O-Pedia: Super Stinky-y Stuff from A to Z.* Walker & Company, 2012

National Graphic Kids *Ultimate Weird but True: 1,000 Wild & Wacky Facts and Photos.* National Geographic Children's Books, 2011

Packard, Mary. *Ripleys Top 10: The Weirdest of the Weird.* Scholastic, 2005

Persels, Jeff and Jeff Russell Ganim. *Fecal Matters in Early Modern Literature and Art: Studies in Scatology.* Ashgate Pub Ltd

Praeger, Dave. *Poop Culture: How America Is Shaped by Its Grossest National Product.* Feral House, 2007

Prager, Ellen. *Sex, Drugs, and Sea Slime: The Oceans' Oddest Creatures and Why They Matter.* University of Chicago Press, 2011

Rockwood, Leigh. *Centipedes and Millipedes Are Gross!* PowerKids Press, 2010

Tahan, Raya. *The Yanomami of South America.* Lerner Publications, 2001

Whitehead, John. *Exploration of Mount Kina Balu, North Borneo.* Gurney and Jackson, 1893

"Consumer Advisory: Only Eat Puffer Fish from Known Safe Sources" FDA U.S. Food & Drug Administration, October 17, 2007

"Pinworm infection" Mayo Clinic; http://www.mayoclinic.com/health/pinworm/DS00687

"The Six Legged Meat of the Future" **Marcel Dicke, Arnold Van Huis,** The Wall Street Journal, 2011

"'Working IX to V' in Ancient Rome and Greece" **Vicki Leon,** npr June 29, 2007, excerpted from *Working IX to V: Orgy Planners, Funeral Clowns, and Other Prized Professions of the Ancient World* by Vicki Leon, Walker & Company, 2007

ILLUSTRATION CREDITS

Cover Illustrations:
Shiny poop © siteflight / www.sxc.hu: *Black widow spider* © Lee Daniels / istockphoto.com: *Leech* © Kevin Green 1/ istockphoto.com: *Cavity* © Ryan Burke / istockphoto.com *Worm and Golden delicious apple* © Adolfo Medina Licon / istockphoto.com: *Piranha* © Ryan Burke / istockphoto.com: *Smiling trash can* © Anthony Oshlick / istockphoto.com: *Bid bad booger ball* © Anthony Oshlick / istockphoto.com: *Sick guy* © Jerry Silvestrini / istockphoto.com: *Evil oil* © Clark McMulle / istockphoto.com: *Mummy walk* © Robert Harness / istockphoto.com *Bed bug* © Larry Rains / istockphoto.com

Interior Illustrations:
All interior illustrations © Chuck Gonzales except for the following:
Icons set Nerds © shutterstock.com: *Cartoon Bugs: Silhouettes* © shutterstock.com: *Splashes* © shutterstock.com: *Cartoon Melting Ice Cream* © shutterstock.com *Vector Illustration: Insect Collection Isolated on White* © shutterstock.com

ACKNOWLEDGMENTS

Thanks to Jeannine Dillon, who had the idea for the book and poured herself into getting the spreads exactly right. She is a great book developer, editor, and friend—equally capable of indulging my complaints about outrageous deadlines and my outrageous dreams about future book plans. Because of this project, neither of us can eat peanut butter anymore.

Thanks to the book's editor, Caitlin Doyle, for her deft and gentle guidance in the revision stages of the manuscript and for her careful copyediting job as well. It is not often that I meet each editor query with a wave of gratitude for having been saved some embarrassment or other.

I'm grateful to Ginny Zeal for the wonderful design, Emily Epstein for proofreading, and Chuck Gonzalez for awesome illustrations that make me laugh and wince in equal measure. It's funny that he and I should partner up again with another contribution to the world of bad manners.

Thanks to my family, who tolerated large swaths of absence last year when the "I'm almost done, just a few more things to do" refrain in the final stages of the first draft lost all connection to reality.

And thanks to my cousin, Will Riordan, who in his preteen years gave me insight into what makes young grossophiles laugh—primarily by entering Christmas celebrations several years in a row squeezing a kind of slimy putty that made an obscene sound.

ABOUT THE AUTHOR

Rachel Federman graduated from Dartmouth College with a degree in English and creative writing and dreams of making an impact within the environmental movement. Shortly after moving to New York City, she was lured by her love of books into the publishing world and worked for many years as an editor and writer by day and a rock musician by night. As a singer, songwriter, and bass player for the indie-rock band Dimestore Scenario, she got to play in lots of great clubs, including CBGB before it closed.

Rachel insists on irritating people by never settling into a full-time job with predictable hours and instead always works part time at various endeavors, including designing programs in minority education for nonprofit organizations, which she's been doing with her father for the past decade. Together, they've written grants and conducted evaluations for over 100 social-justice projects, including disease prevention in West Africa, sustainable development in Nepal, promoting social cohesion in America, and developing creative employment opportunities for U.S. veterans. Her books include *Kiss in the Dark* (Random

House), *Test Your Dog* (Sterling), and *Jiggle Shots* (Abrams). Rachel currently lives in Manhattan, where she tries to balance a freelance writing career with caring for her four-year-old and serving as an advocate for simple, natural childhoods, sustainable living, and community revitalization. In her blog, Last American Childhood, Rachel writes about the New York hyper-parenting scene and her attempts to resist the forces of commercialism that undermine children's imaginations and their appreciation of the natural world. Check it out at: http://lastamericanchildhood.blogspot.com.

ABOUT THE ILLUSTRATOR

Chuck Gonzales works internationally in publishing, editorial, and advertising. His artwork has appeared in such diverse publications as the *New York Times*, *Weekly Reader*, and *Cosmopolitan*, and he has been illustrating the OMG column for *Tiger Beat* for the past ten years. Chuck has also illustrated the Worst Case Scenario Junior series for Chronicle Books in addition to writing and illustrating a graphic novel called *Oscar the Mighty* for Scholastic's Read 180 series. He is fluent in the grotesque obsessions of a 12-year-old mind, and he lives in Brooklyn, New York—where his fluency in the grotesque comes in handy.